WHITE PEAK AIR CRASH SITES

WHITE PEAK AIR CRASH SITES

PAT CUNNINGHAM, DFM

AMBERLEY

First published 2012

Amberley Publishing
The Hill, Stroud
Gloucestershire, GL5 4EP

www.amberleybooks.com

British Library Cataloguing in Publication Data.
A catalogue record for this book is available from the British Library.

ISBN 978 1 4456 0655 2

Typesetting and Origination by Amberley Publishing.
Printed in Great Britain.

CONTENTS

PART TWO: SITES WITH NO SURFACE DEBRIS

PART THREE – APPENDICES

PART FOUR

Introduction

One aim of *White Peak Air Crash Sites* is to supply walkers with the provenance of the aircraft debris they chance upon. Another is to allow them to locate all such sites in the area concerned, that is, from Lichfield north to Buxton; and from Macclesfield east to Chesterfield. Essentially then, the book covers that part of ancient Mercia from low-lying Repton, its capital, to the start of the High-Peak moorland, once home to the Pecsaeton tribe, hence 'Peak'.

The subject matter is air crashes, each of the tragedies illumining the celebrated passage written by Captain A. G. Lamplugh in 1931: 'I am convinced that aviation in itself is not inherently dangerous ... but ... the air ... is terribly unforgiving of any carelessness, incapacity or neglect.' Yet the vast majority of flights are conducted without incident. Indeed, most of the fliers featured in this book departed from their aerodromes alongside others who duly returned safely.

The errors which led to the tragic non-arrivals may vary in detail. In so many cases, however, the courts of inquiry observe, 'pilot descended below cloud when uncertain of his position'. For all too often the aircrews concerned were forced to rely upon dead reckoning – deduced reckoning – for navigation, which any wind change would upset. At the same time, with the pressure altimeter they used being nothing but a barometer, they were unable to determine their actual height above the ground below them. In that era, moreover, the altimeter would be set to read zero before take-off. This meant that, on returning to that take-off location, a reading of 1,000 feet would indicate that much clear air below them. Had they strayed over a 900 foot hill, however, there would be only 100 feet of air below and a blind descent would spell disaster.

Of course, for the great majority a blind descent through cloud meant a white-knuckled moment or two before the destination swam into view. This series deals only with the unlucky few for whom the clouds never did part.

Certainly, any notion of mysterious causes should be discounted from the outset. For virtually every crash detailed was due to human error, so many occurring during the intense period of flying training during the Second World War.

A fundamental difference between the crash sites in the White Peak and those of the Dark – or High – Peak to the north is that they occurred on easily accessible ground where farm work continued the moment the site was cleared. Just the same, it is accepted – albeit reluctantly by this aviator/walker – that many ramblers find no interest in sites lacking visual evidence. So it is that Part One deals with sites where debris, or a memorial, is to be seen, Part Two with sites which, while equally proven, show no evidence. The stories behind the crashes, though, are not a whit less harrowing, while the terrain, more pastoral than rugged, continues to inspire.

This series aims to ensure frustration-free site visits by providing a proven grid reference. Each location has been determined by metal-detector searches backed by contemporary photographs and witness interviews. Just one caveat: with so many White Peak sites situated on farmland the walker will, of course, be meticulous in seeking permission to visit, courtesy counting for so much more than any Right to Roam.

By its nature this book deals with tragedy. It does so, however, from an aviator's non-sentimental standpoint. Even so, there are heroes, each a countryman who, knowing the risks, dared searing heat and imminent explosion in endeavouring to succour the occupants of a crashed machine. The book's dominant standpoint then, holds that anything to do with Flight Safety demands critical evaluation, Criticism – and most especially, Self-Criticism – being as relevant to Aviation as the heartfelt, 'There, but for the Grace of God …' is to the writing of these narratives.

Pat Cunningham, DFM, aviator 1951–1992 and lifelong walker

PART ONE
SITES WITH DEBRIS

1
Wildboarclough

1 BOEING B-17G 43-38944 (SEE FIGS 1–3)
Birchenough Hill (East), Parks Farm Moor, Wildboarclough

SJ 99460 67766 (457 m) impact site and memorial
SJ 99545 67797 (456 m) terminal site
Unit and Station: United States Eighth Army Air Force, 398th Bombardment Group, 603rd
    Bombardment Squadron, AAF131 (RAF Nuthampstead), north-east of Stanstead
Date: 2 January 1945
Crew: five, United States Army Air Force, all killed:
First Lieutenant Donald James DeCleene, pilot
Second Lieutenant Maynard Stravinski, co-pilot
Flight Officer Thomas Manos, navigator
Technical Sergeant Howard F. Ayers, radio operator
Technical Sergeant Frank E. Garry, flight engineer

When detailed to ferry B-17G Flying Fortress 43-38944 from the United States Army Air Force's Base Air Depot at Burtonwood, near Liverpool, to RAF Nuthampstead, near Stanstead, First Lieutenant Donald DeCleene elected to take just five of his ten crew members.

The weather forecast promised a light scattering of cloud with a base lifting from 1,500 feet to 3,000 feet and five miles' visibility. First Lieutenant DeCleene, therefore, elected to fly the 150-mile direct-track route over the intervening high ground. This would have taken the crew under fifty minutes, so it must be assumed that before actually setting course they had carried out a few 'shaking down' exercises, for it was already 1925 hours when their aircraft was seen near Wildboarclough, just 29 miles – 10 minutes' flying time – from Burtonwood.

Both farmer Thomas Smith, at Hammerton Knoll Farm, and farmer Alan Waller, at Blaze Farm, were concerned as the aircraft passed low over their high-moorland holdings with 'its engines roaring steadily' and 'without any indication that it was in difficulties'. Their concern was justified within moments as a flash showed that it had indeed flown into the ground. Striking flat-topped Birchenough Hill at 1,500 feet above sea level, the aircraft burst into flames and slid on, disintegrating and throwing clear the bodies of some of the crew before burning itself out.

The Accident Investigation Committee considered the possibility of an engine failure having caused the machine to turn due east and fly four miles off its direct track to Nuthampstead. With no evidence of such a failure, however, they were forced to find that, 'the plane was operating normally but the pilot was in error due to the extremely low altitude over which he was flying the direct route'.

Visiting the Site

There is opportunity roadside parking just off the A54, beside Leech Wood, below the tee-junction at SJ 99162 68256. Cautiously recrossing the A54 at the junction gives access to a public footpath that runs southerly for 630 yards to pass beneath the northern lip of Birchenough Hill quarry, and the crash site. A standing stone and a commemorative board with collected debris are just feet south of the impact point, but 100 yards to the east there is an extensive scar where the bomber burnt out.

The Seafires' site (see below) is then 450 pathless-yards distant on a heading of 206°M.

2 SUPERMARINE SEAFIRES F Mᴋ 17 SX314, SP325 (see figs 4–5)
Tagsclough Hill, Wildboarclough

SJ 99010 67434 (437 m) SX314 beside wall
SJ 99063 67387 (439 m) SP325
SJ 99202 67385 (439 m) wing debris in gully
Unit and Station: No. 1831 Royal Naval Volunteer Reserve Squadron, HMS *Blackcap*, RN Air
    Station Stretton, south-east of Warrington
Date: 16 July 1949
Crew: pilots, two, killed
Lieutenant Hugh Eccles, Royal Naval Volunteer Reserve (SX314)
Lieutenant Frank James Dyke, Royal Naval Volunteer Reserve (SP325)

On 16 July 1949 two Royal Naval Volunteer Reserve Seafire pilots were killed during a formation exercise when they flew into high ground at Tagsclough Hill, a mile south-east of Wildboarclough.

They had been briefed for a 40-minute sortie to be carried at 2,500 feet to the south of RNAS Stretton. The exercise completed, the leader, Lieutenant Eccles, called for a homing and initial descent, receiving a heading to steer and clearance to 1,500 feet. His response, however, was unusual, 'This is 103 –'. After which nothing more was heard, despite repeated calls.

His response, though truncated, is significant. For had Lieutenant Eccles received the generally northerly steer he anticipated, say 350 degrees, the procedural acknowledgement would have been a terse, 'Three Five Zero, One-Oh-Three: cleared to fifteen hundred feet'. Whereas the discursive, 'This is 103 –,' suggests that he needed time to assess the heading passed, which, from the crash site, would have been effectively westerly. Certainly, there was no suggestion of alarm. Clearly he had no notion that he was twenty miles east of the authorised area.

At the time of this exchange, recorded as 1245 hours, farmer John Robert Lane, of Bennettshitch Farm, was startled when two aircraft in tight formation suddenly appeared from the mist and flew undeviatingly past him, 'At about two yards above the ground,' he told the coroner, 'and five feet from where I was standing …' Transfixed, he saw the machines hit a wall, then flames break out from the one on the right, before both disappeared on into the mist.

Mr Lane's grandson, Mr Thomas Victor Ferns, of Longnor, nodded. 'My grandfather would always say the two planes had been racing, one being slightly ahead of the other [a graphic description of echelon formation!]. I was near the farm with a friend, but although we could tell the planes were very close, and very low, we couldn't see them for the mist and rain. Then we heard this great bang. Immediately we ran up the moor, to find that the wall had been smashed away, leaving furrows, and wreckage, for a good half mile. We found one body, and then another by the far boundary wall. But there was nothing we could do. With flames everywhere, and the smell of burnt rubber ... I just panicked.'

In fact, far from panicking, the youthful Victor did all there was to be done. 'We hadn't a phone at Bennettshitch, so we ran on to the Rose and Crown at Allgreave, where they called the authorities.'

No records of the Royal Naval court of inquiry have come to light, but it is known that the radio-record of Stretton's air traffic control tower was impounded, an act which incensed the coroner. 'The public,' he fulminated, 'ought to know the last words of these airmen ... The court of inquiry had no right ...'

What is clear, however, is that the leader, flying much lower than his authorised minimum height of 2,500 feet, in trying to keep reasonably in the clear, drifted eastwards from the 200 feet or so elevation of Stretton to the misty, 1,500 feet above-sea-level moors of Wildboarclough. It would follow that as the pair impacted at an elevation of 1,433 feet, but with their altimeters still set to register the height above Stretton, Lieutenant Eccles would have expected there to be over a thousand feet of clear air below him. So that with him concentrating on his instrument flying, and with his number two fully intent on holding station, neither realised that they were merely skimming the ground as they flashed past farmer John Lane.

In the aftermath, Mrs Eccles, the mother of Lieutenant Eccles, movingly expressed her thanks for the aid young Victor Ferns had tried to render her son, sending him a New Testament, still a much-prized family memento in 2012.

Visiting the Site

Walkers will probably approach from the nearby B-17 site (see above) and brave the hummock grass. Having done so, visual evidence of the double tragedy was still to be found in 2012 at two of the three associated sites: a mainplane component in a gully, and some 140 yards west, a small debris pool where SP325 came to rest, with the wall which finally stopped SX314 just 130 yards north-west of that.

2

The Roaches

3 JUNKERS JU 88-A5 No. 6213 (SEE FIGS 6–8)
Roach End, The Roaches

SK 00407 64710 (319 m)
Unit and Station: Luftwaffe *Kampfgeschwader* (Bomber Group) No. 76, Leuwarden
    (Netherlands's north coast, due east of Norwich)
Date: 8 May 1941
Crew: four, all killed
Major Dietrich Von Ziehlberg, pilot [Squadron Leader]
Oberleutnant Walter Lembke, observer [Flying officer]
Oberfeldwebel Rudolf Schwalbe, wireless operator [Flight sergeant]
Feldwebel Georg Mahl, air gunner [Sergeant]

On the night of 8 May 1941 Junkers Ju 88s of *Kampfgeschwader* No. 76 were tasked to bomb the Liverpool docks. *Major* Von Ziehlberg duly made his attack, but shortly after turning for home his wireless operator called the rest of the force to advise that they were baling out of their blazing aircraft. They left it too late, however, for although one crew member was poised at the escape exit the aircraft crashed into a hillside at Roach End, killing all four men aboard.

Former Home Guard Ernest Bowyer was among those who hurried to the scene. He recalled, 'We found a propeller, then the body of a German airman. The front of the aircraft had totally burnt out, leaving only the rear section. This contained two more bodies and was riddled with bullet holes. An RAF officer told us that one crew member was unaccounted for, so we began searching further along the valley. We found the escape hatch, and belts of bullets, but no airman. On returning to the aircraft, however, the officer clambered over a large cinder pile. I made to follow, but then hesitated. And finally told him that he had, in fact, found the missing airman.'

Mrs Christine Chester, née Snow, then of Wolf Dale Farm, Rudyard Lake, was another early visitor to the scene. 'There was burnt wreckage everywhere, and they hadn't even removed the bodies.' She paused, then observed, 'It was ugly. But I felt no sympathy. Those airmen would not be bombing the people of Liverpool again. And a dead enemy was a good thing …'

Visiting the Site

The closest, if limited, roadside parking offers at SJ 99560 64494, after which a well-worth-walking path descends north-eastwards to Black Brook. From the bridge at SJ 00300 64714 the easiest passage is to angle up towards the tree line on 092°M for 112 yards. Even so, heather may conceal the scanty molten masses that remained in 2012.

4 AVRO LANCASTER B Mk 1 NF908 (see figs 9–11)
The Roaches

SK 00155 63600 (487 m)
Unit and Station: No. 467 Squadron, Royal Australian Air Force, RAF Waddington, south of
    Lincoln, No. 5 Group, Bomber Command
Date: 3 January 1945
Crew: seven, all killed
Flying Officer Walter Vernon Wilfred Allamby, RAAF, pilot
Flight Lieutenant Jack Ivan Pritchard, RAAF, navigator
Flight Sergeant Geoffrey James Dunbar, RAAF, bomb aimer
Flight Sergeant Richard Emonson, RAAF, wireless operator
Flight Sergeant Norman Lees, RAF Volunteer Reserve, flight engineer
Flight Sergeant Thomas Edward Harold Wright, RAAF, air gunner
Flight Sergeant Cleveland Charles Watson, RAAF, air gunner, rear turret

When Flying Officer Walter Allamby and his predominantly Australian crew were detailed for a combined navigation and fighter-affiliation sortie, they were especially briefed to maintain a minimum height of 4,000 feet. While still 58 miles from Waddington, however, their Lancaster was flown into The Roaches at just 1,600 feet above sea level, exploding in flames and killing all on board.

Finding no evidence of a malfunction, the inquiry concluded that Flying Officer Allamby had decided to let down blind through cloud. As a radio fix could easily have been obtained, the court submitted that Flying Officer Allamby had disobeyed orders, thereby causing the loss of his aircraft and his crew.

Visiting the Site

The closest roadside parking, though limited, is at SJ 99560 64494, 0.66 miles from the crash site. The latter lies along the must-be-walked Roaches Spine, just below the ridge, and 310 yards east of the 505-m trig column. By 2012 there was little sizeable debris, although molten fragments silvered several burnt patches.

3

Merryton Low

5 LOCKHEED P-38J LIGHTNING 42-67670 (SEE FIGS 12–13)
Merryton Low, north-east of Leek

SK 03509 61510 (440 m) Impact site
SK 04200 60980 (484 m) Pilot landed
SK 04405 60890 (470 m) Canopy fell
Unit and Station: United States Eighth Army Air Force, 310th Ferrying Squadron, AAF582
   (RAF Warton), 27th Air Transport Group, 8th Air Force Service Command
Date: 22 December 1943
Crew: pilot, baled out, suffered abrasions
Second Lieutenant Guy A. Senesac, USAAF

Just eleven days after forced-landing a faulty P-38J Lightning (see page 25 below), Second Lieutenant Guy Senesac was tasked to deliver another of the twin-boomed, twin-engined, long-range escort fighters to an American unit at RAF King's Cliffe, just west of Peterborough. He was to route south to Chester before taking up a south-easterly heading. Increasing amounts of low cloud, however, forced him to turn much sooner than he had planned. After a while, accordingly, finding himself in thick cloud with just 600 feet indicated on his altimeter, he decided to turn back.

He was very honest in his post-crash report, readily admitting that, even as he turned, so the unassuaged nervousness from his recent forced-landing swept over him, and he lost control. He tried to climb, but his vertical speed indicator seemed to show that he was descending rapidly. As he wrote, 'Not being very high, I immediately opened the canopy, and jumped … My chute had no sooner opened than I hit the ground. It knocked the wind out of me …' In addition, he suffered bruising and abrasions as the wind dragged him. Regarding his aircraft, he wrote, 'the local bobbies say it is a total wreck.'

As Mr Cyril Swain, of Swainsmoor Farm, remembered, 'We were used to Wellingtons droning over and showering us with cartridge cases as they let fly at drogues towed by Lysanders. But we didn't see American Lightnings every day. Yet I recognised it at once. It dived almost vertically into the ground above Strines Farm, then exploded. There wasn't that much of a crater, and not many large parts – but there were belts of ammunition.' He smiled. 'And we'd make rings out of perspex and from aluminium tubing ...'

'The pilot', Mr Swain elaborated, 'came down on the actual top. For Charlie, my brother, found the canopy along the Warslow road, just beyond Blake Mere.'

Having been medically checked in Leek, Second Lieutenant Senesac had awaited air transport at RAF Ashbourne, where a British airman recalled this accident-prone ally drawling, 'A hell of a coincidence', connecting this episode to his so recent mishap.

The Britisher noted too, a little sourly, 'He hadn't done a single operational trip, yet his tunic was festooned with medal ribbons.'

The accident investigators were not unduly harsh in their conclusions, recording that Second Lieutenant Senesac had lost control of his aircraft 'due to a momentary lapse of proficiency exacerbated by the excited state of his mind'.

It is to be hoped that things went somewhat better for him – and the Allies – on his next flight!

Visiting the Site

It is probable that this site will be visited after that of Stirling N6075 (below). Convenient parking for both off-path sites offers at SK 04009 61319, where a track leads into the moor. From the rim immediately above the Stirling site the P-38 lies 214 yards off, on the same contour, walking on 066°M. By 2012 the crater, sited above Strines Farm, had become a hump, but scraps of surface debris were still evident.

6 SHORT STIRLING Mk 1 N6075 (SEE FIG 14)
Merryton Low, north-east of Leek

SK 03798 61169 (436 m)
Unit and Station: No. 101 Squadron Conversion Flight, RAF Oakington, north-west of
    Cambridge, No. 3 Group, Bomber Command
Date: 13 July 1942
Crew: seven, plus one passenger, all killed
Sergeant Roderick Urquhart Morrison, RAF Volunteer Reserve, pilot
Flight Sergeant John Richard Griffin, Royal Canadian Air Force, observer
Flight Sergeant James Frederick Hirst, RCAF, wireless operator/air gunner
Flight Sergeant Thorstein Enevold Helgesen, RCAF, wireless operator/air gunner
Sergeant de Section (Flight Sergeant) Leo Joseph Regimbal, RCAF, air gunner: mortally injured
Flight Sergeant John Ellis Williams, RAFVR, staff flight engineer
Sergeant William Anthony George Atkins, RAFVR, pupil flight engineer
Flight Sergeant Edgar Dolphin, RAFVR, passenger

Sergeant Roderick Morrison and his crew had been airborne for four hours when they arrived in the Biddulph area, 115 miles from Oakington, and spent some time circling low over their passenger's house. Such unauthorised low flying has always been an indictable offence, nevertheless it was a commonplace practice, and innocuous enough. Always provided things went well. However, when Sergeant Morrison turned for base he entered a cloud-topped gully on Merryton Low, crashed, and killed everyone on board.

Farm workers reaching the site found that the Stirling had impacted flatly up the slope, breaking into sections, with the fuel and oil igniting. They managed to extricate the rear gunner from the detached tail section, but he died shortly afterwards.

Mr Eric Williams, of Cherry Tree Farm, was near The Mermaid Inn, high on the crest, when the crash occurred. 'It was very foggy at that height,' he recalled, 'and when we got there it seemed everything was on fire. It was clear that he'd just flown too low, and hadn't seen the hill … They were foreigners, I believe …'

The RAF field investigators reported that, 'The accident was caused by the pilot flying too low in cloud in the region of high ground whilst trying to locate the house of the passenger's wife.' The more formal court of inquiry, however, while conceding that, 'the finding of the investigators may be right,' submitted that it considered a 'more correct finding to be, error of airmanship by the pilot who flew unnecessarily low over high ground in bad weather.' A finding ratified by higher authority.

Visiting the Site

Convenient parking offers at SK 04009 61319 where a track leads off into the moor. The debris pool is then 270 yards off-path on 229°M. Descending into the actual gully requires care, so save the magnificent view of the Roaches until firm-footed once again. In 2012 several scraps had been gathered, but diligent searching discovered more in the deep heather.

7 HAWKER HURRICANE Mk 1 V6793 (see figs 15–16)
Fleet Green, east of Merryton Low

SK 04740 61317 (415 m)
Unit and Station: No. 5 (Pilots) Advanced Flying Unit, RAF Ternhill, south-west of Market
    Drayton, No. 21 Group, Flying Training Command
Date: 27 July 1944
Crew: Pilot, killed
Flight Sergeant Roswell Howard Tourle Martin, Royal New Zealand Air Force

When pupil pilot Flight Sergeant Roswell Martin was detailed to carry out aerobatics 'above 5,000 feet' together with local-area familiarisation, he had 130 hours solo but just four on the Hurricane. After forty minutes Flight Sergeant Martin's gyrations had carried him over cloud-covered Merryton Low, only he then began a manoeuvre that took him almost vertically into the ground.

The inquiry found that Flight Sergeant Martin had failed to maintain his briefed minimum-safe-altitude for aerobatics. They would further have reasoned that he had been misled by his altimeter, which had been set for Ternhill (269 feet above sea level) and would have been showing a handsome – and totally false – margin of height over the 1,600-foot Merryton Low. They also deduced that Flight Sergeant Martin had entered cloud during his final manoeuvre, and failing to realise that he was inverted, had pulled back on the stick, nosing himself into moorland barely 700 feet below.

As Mr George Deaville, of Lower Fleetgreen Farm, would recall, 'The young chap had obviously dived in nose first, for he'd made such a deep crater. It wasn't pretty.'

Visiting the Site

Careful parking offers off the Morridge road on the gravel loop at SK 04242 61064. The site then lies some 600 yards downhill, and very off-path, on a heading of 057°M, a rushy ditch (not the wall shown on the map!) giving the line until the last 160 yards. In 2012 there was a small pool of debris in the still-sizeable grassy crater.

4

Rudyard

8 SHORT STIRLING Mк 3 LK502 (see figs 17–18)
Cliffe Park, Rudyard

SJ 93955 59812 (190 m)

Unit and Station: No. 1654 Heavy Conversion Unit, RAF Wigsley, west of Lincoln, No. 5 Group, Bomber Command

Date: 27 May 1944

Crew: eight, four killed

Flying Officer Gordon Noble Leach, pilot, killed, parachute failed to open, fell between Rudyard Lake and crash site (SJ 94000 5990 [200 m])

Flight Sergeant Geoffrey Norman Wise, navigator, unhurt, parachuted into field above Wolf Dale Farm (SJ 94380 61230 [250 m])

Flight Sergeant D. C. Watson, bomb-aimer, parachuted into field below Lake View Garage (SJ 94580 60130 [187 m])

Flight Sergeant Bernard David Fine, RAAF, wireless operator, killed

Flight Sergeant Frederick Thomas James Nicholls, flight engineer, parachuted between Dingle Brook and the lake feeder conduit (SJ 93960 60990 [160 m]), injured, but rescued from the mud and taken to Wolf Dale Farm

Flight Sergeant Arthur C. Brett, pupil flight engineer, parachuted into field at Birch Trees Farm (SJ 93600 59430 [220 m])

Sergeant Harold Ward, air gunner, killed

Sergeant Charles David Howes, air gunner, killed

One of the complexities involved in converting to four-engined heavy bombers was learning to control them when an engine was lost. Essentially, a stopped engine acts like a brake and pulls the nose sideways towards it. This 'yawing' motion results in the unaffected wing, with both its engines still live, forging ahead and creating additional lift. This extra lift, however, sets up a rolling motion which, combining with the sideways motion of the nose, produces a spiral dive. The aim, then, is to contain the sideways yaw before the spiral dive develops.

Another quite different problem could arise, however, on restarting an engine which had been stopped as a drill, for it was vital to address the correct engine …

On the night of 27 May 1944, Flying Officer Gordon Leach and his mainly trainee crew had been airborne for nearly four and a half hours and were just fifty miles from base. The ideal opportunity, therefore, to practise stopping an engine. And so the starboard-inner was stopped, and the propeller 'feathered': its blades being turned edgewise-on, as with an oar, to minimise the drag.

Stopping and feathering an inner engine would have eased the crew gently into the drill, for an inner, with its shorter moment arm, causes less swing than an outer. And having trimmed the aircraft to its new configuration, and with both pilot and pupil flight engineer satisfied that they had gleaned all the exercise had to offer, the starboard-inner would have been started up again.

Only here the pupils were to make what was to prove a fatal error. For inadvertently the starboard-outer engine was cut, leaving the Stirling on its two port engines. And now Flying Officer Leach had his hands really full. But not only his hands – desperately trying to roll on yet more left bank to stem the lifting left wing – but one foot as well, on the left rudder, straining to counteract the sideways pull to the right.

And because the propeller controls were positioned low to his right at the very bottom of the control box, and with him over busy trying to physically recover, *on instruments*, from the spiral, he had little spare capacity for the re-starting of either stopped engine.

Nor, tragically, with his right leg lending purchase to his straining left leg, his arms rigid, forcing the wheel hard over, and his torso blocking so much access, was it easy for either his flight engineer or the staff flight engineer to usefully render assistance. On top of that it was night, over a blacked-out land, and with the speed – and therefore the noise level! – more alarmingly winding up with every flustered moment.

It was by no means an irrecoverable situation, but lacking experience, Flying Officer Leach found himself quite unable to regain control, and ordered the crew to abandon.

Only the order had been given woefully late. Just the same, four of them descended safely. But pilot Flying Officer Leach's own parachute failed to open due to lack of height, while his spiralling aircraft, with three crew still aboard, impacted and exploded on the western shore of Rudyard Reservoir.

Of the successful jumpers, two found succour at Wolf Dale Farm, across the road to the east of the reservoir, a third at what was then a garage, also on the eastern shore, and the fourth in farmland beyond the crash site. But of these four, fortunate as they were on this occasion, all bar Flight Sergeant Watson, the bomb aimer, were subsequently to be killed on operations.

The court of inquiry had little to do, for exchanges over the intercom had made it evident that while attempting the starboard-inner re-start, the starboard-outer had been inadvertently stopped instead. The court tendered, however, that the pilot had probably not received the best of training, had therefore operated the wrong lever, stopped the other engine on the starboard side, and subsequently lost control.

The Air Officer Commanding-in-Chief concurred with the findings, but pressed too, 'The provision of engine loss-of-power warning lights … is urgently needed.'

How many aircrew since would have blessed his name had that urgent need only been met!

Mr Freddie Brown, of Barnswood Farm, saw the blazing aircraft from his bedroom window. 'There were lights, and explosions, and people shouting,' he remembered. 'All very disturbing to a six-year old.'

Thirteen-year-old Christine Snow (to become Mrs Christine Chester) of Wolf Dale Farm smiled, 'The heroine of the night was Dolly, Mrs Gibson. Her husband was on night duty but when she heard shouts, and a whistle blowing, she went out into the marsh, eventually discovering one of the aircrew, virtually entombed in thick mud. Though Dolly was only slightly built, by sheer persistence she finally tugged him free, then managed to walk him to our place, which had a telephone.'

Mrs Chester remembered that when the bedraggled pair arrived at her parents' farm, her father poured the airman a glass of whisky only to find that the man – Flight Sergeant Nicholls, the staff flight engineer – would accept nothing but a cup of tea. After a while, however, there was a knock at the door, and navigator Geoffrey Wise appeared, 'The most glamorous of young men,' Mrs Chester remembered fondly. 'He saw the glass of whisky, walked across, and drained it. "You know," he said then, "first, I have to bale out. Then I land in a herd of cows! – certain that the bull would be along to finish me off." Poor man, worried about a bull, not realising he'd only narrowly missed the 33,000 volt power lines!'

American troops had been camped on the lakeside below Cliffe Park Hall (then a youth hostel), to practice driving specially adapted lorries over perforated-steel-plate 'roadways' sunk in the water. 'They were practising for the Invasion,' Mrs Chester remembered, 'as it turned out, only days away! But that night [it would have been their shouting Freddie Brown heard!] they turned on all their headlights to floodlight the area. Only there was nothing they could do to help.'

Mrs Chester produced a sketch map showing where each of the parachuting aircrew had landed. 'I drew this,' she explained, 'having taken my horse out at first light to see if I could find anyone else.' Pausing, she recalled, 'The pilot, having baled out too late, had made a sizeable hole.'

Though rescuer Mrs Dolly Gibson had truly shone on that fateful night, any form of public recognition was to be long in coming. In October 1990, however, a memorial to all German and Allied airmen killed in the area was unveiled in Leek, and her heroism was finally recognised. 'If only,' Mrs Chester smiled, 'with a bunch of flowers, and a kiss from our locally-grown Air Chief Marshal.'

Visiting the Site

The nearest public parking is some three quarters of a mile off at SJ 93931 61129, from which an initially metalled road leads around the end of the lake. The meadows on a direct line to the site are enticing, but the woods beyond mask deep swamps. Best, then, to stay on the road-cum-path and pass just below Cliffe Park Hall. After which, continuing on the path for 200 yards (to SJ 93959 59836) leaves the site just 80 feet upslope. In 2012 a small cache of surface debris remained.

5

Leek

9 REPUBLIC P-47C THUNDERBOLT 41-6628 (SEE FIGS 19–20)
Easing Farm, Thorncliffe, Leek

SK 02095 57789 (340 m)

Unit and Station: United States Eighth Army Air Force, 8th Fighter Command, 495th Fighter Training Group, AAF342 (RAF Atcham, south-east of Shrewsbury)

Date: 3 October 1944

Crew: pilot, killed

Second Lieutenant Quentin J. Sella, USAAF

On 3 October 1944 Second Lieutenant Quentin J. Sella was detailed as one of a four-ship formation detailed to carry out, initially, formation flying in cloudy conditions, and then battle formation. After take-off, the leader headed north-eastwards for some forty miles to utilise a mass of cloud near Leek. Flying at 3,000 feet, he next took the formation in a series of gentle, predominately-climbing penetrations, entering cloud for some while, then turning back into clear air once again. The formation adopted was what the RAF would have known as a 'Right-handed section finger-four' which, when widened out, provided good operational flexibility. When held close, however, it meant that all three formating pilots were fully occupied in maintaining station on some part of the neighbouring machine held hovering only inches from their own. Undoubtedly the most demanding position was that held by Lieutenant Sella, the number four, for the least twitch of the number three – formating directly on the leader – magnified the correction required to maintain station.

There came a time, though, when the pilot on the leader's left – his number two – called that he had lost station. The leader immediately issued him with a climbing course which would fan him clear of the others. And on once more breaking cloud moments later, the stray was seen a safe two miles off to the left.

In the interim however, the number three, to the leader's immediate right, had experienced momentary difficulties. So had he twitched? For an instant later, Second Lieutenant Sella, desperately trying to hold station on him, called that he was breaking. The leader gave him too a suitable spacing heading which was promptly acknowledged. Only there was no further contact.

The leader was not unduly concerned, for a follower becoming detached was not uncommon, but as radio calls went unacknowledged he descended, anticipating that the missing aircraft had emerged from cloud lower down. However, on finding the cloud base only some five hundred feet above the hills, and dark with rain besides, he climbed his depleted section back into the clear and fulfilled the battle-formation element of the sortie.

As it was, Second Lieutenant Sella had been unable to adapt to finding himself so abruptly obliged to revert to flight on instruments alone and, losing control, had fallen into a near-vertical dive. He had managed to jettison his canopy, clearly intending to evacuate, but the air rush had prevented this, so that his seven-ton machine had carried him with it, plunging into marshy moorland.

At the investigation the other pilots confirmed that no manoeuvres had been carried out that were likely to topple the gyroscope of an artificial horizon, the main attitude indicator. However, the investigators still felt that Second Lieutenant Sella's artificial horizon might not have not been fully stabilised. Even so, they decided, he should then have reverted more swiftly to interpreting his basic instruments. They also observed that had he made more effort he would not have lost the formation in the first place, when the state of his gyros would have been immaterial: a trifle hard, perhaps, considering that the number two had similarly broken formation, and without a twitchy intervening machine to make his station-keeping task harder!

The investigators, pilots themselves, also felt that had Second Lieutenant Sella been more decisive, and jumped before the speed built up too much, his evacuation would have been successful. Again, a hard-skinned view, but one which reflects the undeviating standard of criticism – self-criticism – applied throughout aviation.

The crater, on Easing Farm, at Thorncliffe, was so deep, and the ground so wet, that the decision was eventually made to leave Second Lieutenant Sella's body interred, together with much of the aircraft. In 2012 scraps of debris continued to emerge through the red, clayey mud.

Visiting the Site

A public footpath running between Easing Lane and Morridge – with opportunity roadside parking at each end – passes the rushy site. In 2012 debris was gathered at a white cross with a not-that-appropriately-worded plaque.

6

Grindon

10 HANDLEY PAGE HALIFAX Mᴋ 9 RT922 (ꜱᴇᴇ ꜰɪɢꜱ 21–24)
Grindon, Staffordshire

SK 06273 55320 (352 m)
Unit and Station: No. 47 Squadron, RAF Fairford, No. 38 Group, Transport Command
Date: 13 February 1947
Occupants: eight, two civilian passengers, six crew; all killed:
Crew:
Squadron Leader Donald McIntyre, pilot
Flight Lieutenant Ernest Smith, navigator
Warrant Officer Gordon Victor Chapman, navigator
Warrant Officer Richard Sidney Kearns, flight engineer
Flight Sergeant Kenneth Charles Pettit, wireless operator
Warrant Officer W. Sherry, despatcher
Passengers:
Mr J. Reardon, press photographer
Mr D. W. Savill, press photographer

In the winter of 1947 many isolated communities in the British Isles were cut off by snow. It is held, however, that pressure from local nurses for powdered baby milk led to aerial supply drops being organised for the Staffordshire villages of Longnor and Grindon. The initial drop at Longnor saw 20,000 lb of supplies delivered. 'The weather was poor,' said Mr John Bradbury of Folds Farm, Longnor. 'Still, they dropped the parachutes, although one bundle burst …'

A day later, Squadron Leader Donald McIntyre also encountered poor conditions, with so much cloud covering Grindon Moor that he had difficulty in locating the dropping-zone identifier, a cross of soot. Certainly, such conditions would have made even an operational air-supply drop extremely problematical. Indeed, the operations order had specifically laid down a minimum dropping height of 1,500 feet above ground level, a stricture reinforced at the pre-departure briefing. Squadron Leader McIntyre, however, with almost 2,000 hours' flying experience and 400 on Halifaxes, decided against aborting the drop.

He made two unsuccessful runs at gradually descending heights, and began a third. Only this time he approached so low that as he banked to correct his line-up, the starboard wing touched a slope and cartwheeled his aircraft into the ground, where it exploded and burnt, killing all on board.

Farmer Mr Arthur Coates remembered, 'It was filthy weather, and I was helping clear snow from the bend in Parsons Lane, beside the field they were using. Only as the aircraft passed overhead this time it began to turn. And that's when it touched its wing …' He paused, then added soberly, 'That same day the bread van was able to get through, and the local nurse.'

The RAF court of inquiry had no option but to find that the pilot had disobeyed his orders in descending as low as he did; also by failing to abort the drop on finding poor visibility and a 100-foot cloud base. It observed too that once airborne, the urgency of the task had been exaggerated. But it recorded as well that an updated actual-weather report might have led Transport Command Operations, the authorising formation, to cancel the sortie. No such intervention occurring, zeal to accomplish the task took over.

Squadron Leader McIntyre's son, Mr Donald 'Grem' McIntyre – his given name, 'Grem' derives from 'Gremlin', the mischief-makers who delighted in bringing woe to wartime aircraft – later corresponded with aircrew who had flown with his father, a correspondence redolent with the flavour of those times when the Second World War had so recently finished and the 'press-on' spirit still prevailed. Indeed, participant aircrew told him that even the previous day's supply drop to Longnor, piloted by the squadron's commanding officer, had been forced to pull up to avoid a bridge in near-whiteout conditions not too dissimilar from those obtaining at the Grindon drop.

A very positive legacy of the Grindon tragedy, however, is that thanks to stiffened safety rulings, transport-operations casualties in all post-war theatres diminished dramatically.

Visiting the Site
Both crash site and memorial are on land belonging to New House Farm, access being by a footpath off Parsons Lane at SK 06773 55330 and signposted '47 Squadron Cairn'. This, though, offers no sensible parking. Permission could be sought, however, to park on the lay-by opposite the farm and to utilise the adjacent cart track. The monument is then 300 yards distant, the track passing the now ruinous barn (at SK 06432 55413) where the crash victims were laid. The Halifax impacted in the fields faced by the monument, but emergent surface debris is rare.

7

Monyash

11 LOCKHEED P-38J LIGHTNING 42-67480 (SEE FIGS 25–26)
Cronkstone Low, north-west of Sparklow

SK 11539 66057 (365 m) touchdown site
SK 11495 66139 (368 m) terminal site, wall
Unit and Station: United States Eighth Army Air Force, 310th Ferrying Squadron, AAF582
    (RAF Warton), 27th Air Transport Group, 8th Air Force Service Command
Date: 11 December 1943
Crew: pilot, survived single-engined forced-landing
Second Lieutenant Guy A. Senesac, USAAF

On 11 December 1943 Second Lieutenant Guy Senesac was tasked to deliver a twin-boomed, twin-engined P-38J Lightning to its operational unit at RAF King's Cliffe, just west of Peterborough. He was halfway to his destination, flying at 1,000 feet, when his right-hand engine stopped. He immediately checked his fuel and ignition but was unable to effect a re-start.

'I increased the power on my good engine,' Second Lieutenant Senesac reported, 'and attempted to drop [the] belly tanks but they would not release.'

Even having feathered the windmilling propeller he found that he was still losing height, so decided to land at the first airfield he came across. Within minutes, however, when the good engine objected to such heavy usage, he decided to put the machine on the ground without delay.

'I headed,' his report continued, 'for an open field that I spotted just over my right engine. My altitude was only two hundred feet at this time and I just had time to turn into the field and land wheels up. I hit the ground at about 150 miles per hour, slid about one hundred yards and crashed into a stone wall.'

Second Lieutenant Senesac vacated the cockpit, and running uphill, jumped another drystone wall just as the machine burst into flames and ammunition began exploding. At the same moment, he became aware of shouting, and peering over the wall, caught sight of would-be rescuers coming his way.

Mrs Irene Cole, then of Cronkstone Grange Farm, remembered the story her brothers had returned with. 'As they got close they saw his hand waving to tell them to take cover. So they joined him, and kept their heads down until things quietened.'

Among those sheltering was young Alan Grindy, of Longnor, visiting relatives at Cronkstone Grange Farm. 'The pilot,' he said, 'had shucked off his parachute pack as he ran, but now wanted to save it. Cousin Frank jumped up, but with so many bullets going off he quickly dropped down again, so the flames got it. "That'll be another thing I'll have to pay for then," the pilot joked.'

At length Second Lieutenant Senesac was escorted down to the Grange, a stately farmhouse, lamentably long-since demolished. 'He was very shocked,' Mrs Cole remembered, 'but he took a great interest when I started cooking ham and eggs …' She smiled. 'For me, of course, there was the feeling that this had all happened before. RAF and Poles in 1942 with the Lysander (see page 77, below), and now RAF and American Air Force. The RAF came from their Harpur Hill depot, near Buxton, and were billeted with us until they had cleared the field but I hung on to a great bar of molten aluminium for many a year.'

The investigators charged that poor technique had caused the remaining engine to overheat. Only one wonders if Second Lieutenant Senesac inwardly queried how long they had pored over the manuals before deciding that he, in the limited time available to him, had shown himself lacking … But at least, as he must have consoled himself, he was alive. And had lived to fly another day.

Except that just eleven days later he would leave a second P-38 in flames! (see page 17, above).

Visiting the Site

From the opportunity roadside parking at SK 11382 65573 on the Sparklow–Crowdecote road, a footpath runs northerly beside a wood and after 500 yards passes 180 yards from the drystone wall in which, if anywhere, surface debris might be found. In 2012, the wall was ruinous, with just the section rebuilt after the crash still standing.

*1 Boeing B-17G, Birchenough Hill (East)
See page 13*

Top: **1.** Boeing B-17 bomber.

Middle: **2.** The impact site of B-17G 43-38944, looking towards Shutlingshoe.

Bottom: **3.** The terminal site, looking back along the line of flight.

Supermarine Seafires, Tagsclough Hill
See page *14*

Left: **4.** Supermarine Seafire.

Below: **5.** Debris from Seafires SX314 and SP325 in the gully site, looking towards Gradbach Hill.

Jumkers Ju 88, Tagsclough Hill
See page 15

6. (Inset) Junkers Ju 88.

Above: **7.** The debris pool from Ju 88-A5 No. 6213.

Below: **8.** Looking from the crash site towards Black Brook bridge.

Avro Lancaster, The Roaches
See page 16

9. (Inset) Avro Lancaster.

Above: **10.** The impact site of Lancaster NF908, spreading upslope towards The Roaches ridge path.

Below: **11.** Walkers at the impact site examining debris.

Lockheed P-38 Lightning, Merryton Low
See page 17

12. Lockheed P-38 Lightning.

13. The impact site of P-38 42-67670, above Strines Farm, looking towards Hen Cloud.

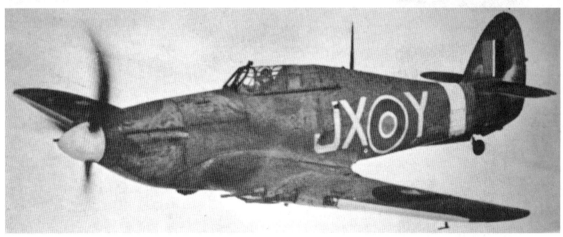

Stirling N0675, Merryton Low
See page 18

Opposite above: **14.** The terminal site of
Short Stirling N6075, overlooking the
impact slope towards Hen Cloud.

Hawker Hurricane Mk 1 V6793, Fleet Green
See page 19

Opposite below: **15.** Hawker Hurricane.

Right: **16.** The impact site of Hurricane
V6793, looking towards Upper Fleet Green
Farm.

Short Stirling Mk 3 LK502, Cliffe Park
See page 20

Below: **17.** Walkers, and an unimpressed
dog, examine debris from Stirling LK502,
with Cliffe Park beyond.

18. (Inset) Surface debris from LK502,
2012.

Republic P-47C Thunderbolt, Easing Farm, Thorncliffe
See page 22

Above: **19.** The memorial cross to the pilot of Thunderbolt 41-6628, looking towards Ashes Farm.

Below: **20.** The parachute deploys after its forty-five-year interment.

Handley Page Halifax, Grindon, Staffordshire
See page 24

21. Handley Page Halifax showing the original shape of the tailfin's leading edge.

22. (Inset) The modified quadrilateral shape which helped overcome a serious stability problem.

23. The impact site of Halifax RT922, looking towards the memorial, 2012.

24. (Inset) The memorial.

Lockheed P-38 Lightning, Cronkstone Low
See page 25

25. The terminal area, and beyond, the walls where the pilot and the would-be rescuers took shelter.

26. Surface debris from 42-67480, examined, then secreted in wall.

8
Youlgreave

12 VICKERS WELLINGTON Mᴋ 3 BJ652 (ꜱᴇᴇ ꜰɪɢꜱ 27–29)
Smerrill Grange, Middleton

SK 19948 62065 (205 m)
SK 19559 63182 memorial plaque, in Middleton
Unit and Station: No. 27 Operational Training Unit, RAF Lichfield, No. 93 Group, Bomber
    Command
Date: 21 January 1944
Crew: six, Royal Australian Air Force, all killed
Flight Sergeant Lloyd George Edmonds, pilot
Flying Off Keith Jobson Perrett, navigator
Flight Sergeant James Kydd, bomb aimer
Flight Sergeant Frederick Popsham Deshon, staff wireless operator
Flight Sergeant William Thomas Barnes, wireless operator
Sergeant Thomas Dudley Murton, air gunner

When Flight Sergeant Lloyd Edmonds and his all-Australian trainee crew were dispatched on a night cross-country exercise, periodical W/T contacts – position reports, weather updates, fixes and bearings – attested to the fact that there were no navigational problems. However, towards the end of the sortie the aircraft ran into cloud.

Whether Flight Sergeant Edmonds experienced difficulty in making the transition onto flight by instruments and began an almost imperceptible descent or whether, despite the blacked-out terrain, he tried to stay visual just below the cloud base can never be known for certain. But one villager in Middleton was so alarmed at how low the aircraft was flying that he hurried out to gaze after it.

And indeed, just moments later, although the aircraft was on course for RAF Church Broughton, it entered the curved ravine carrying Rowlow Brook and impacted at cruising speed into a crag below its rim.

On reaching the scene, Mr Colin Rowland, on leave from the Irish Guards, joined a policeman and members of the Gregory family from Smerrill Grange Farm – above the rim, but otherwise just yards along the projected flight path! – in extricating the bodies and carrying them to the nearest barn. Except that with five men laid out, the RAF authorities advised that one remained unaccounted for.

The would-be rescue party once more clambered down to the site, this time realising that the tail, teetering from the crag, held both the rear turret and the missing gunner. 'The policeman,' Guardsman Rowland said soberly, 'thought the airman might be still alive. But when I reached up, his boot came away in my hand …'

The investigating officers submitted that the accident was due to the pilot failing to appreciate from his instrument scan that he was in a gradual descent. And with higher authority concurring, the incident was closed. At least, until 1995, when a modest memorial was erected in nearby Middleton.

Visiting the Site

The site lies on Merrill Grange Farm, but with permission given, direct access is possible, although involving the careful scaling of the drystone wall demolished by, then rebuilt by, the RAF salvage crew. Alternatively, parking is available in Middleton, when branching off the Bradford Dale path at SK 19678 63178 and following subsequent tracks will access the Rowlow Brook ravine at SK 20028 62478. After that, a shooters' track runs along the brook, passing beneath the site at SK 19992 62092. The upwards slope is steep and seasonally overgrown, but it would be unusual not to find sections of geodetic airframe. This route can be made circular by following the ravine to the far end – there is a deserted village nearby! – then climbing up and left, back to Middleton.

9

Wirksworth

13 BRISTOL BLENHEIM Mᴋ 5 AZ876 (ꜱᴇᴇ ꜰɪɢꜱ 30–32)
Hillcliff Farm, Idridgehay

SK 29599 47544 (89 m)
Unit and Station: No. 42 Operational Training Unit, RAF Ashbourne, Air Defence of Great
    Britain Command, formerly No. 70 (Army Co-operation) Group
Date: 9 July 1943
Crew: three, all killed
Flying Officer Michael Mathew, RAF Volunteer Reserve, pilot
Flying Officer Robert Andrew Whitmore, RAFVR, navigator/air bomber
Sergeant Frederick Harry Doe, RAFVR, wireless operator/air gunner

Flying Officer Michael Mathew and his trainee crew had embarked upon a night cross-country flight that was to culminate in a bombing practice at the nearby Carsington Range. Just fifteen minutes after take-off, however, their aircraft dived near-vertically into the ground at Hillcliff Farm, Idridgehay, exploding, burning out, and killing all three crew members.

The aircraft had fragmented so badly that the investigators welcomed input from two witnesses. One, a member of the Royal Observer Corps, reported that the aircraft, flying at some 3,000 feet, turned right before entering a vertical dive. The other added that both engines were running normally, but held that a sudden nose drop had preceded the dive.

The investigators considered three possibilities: that Flying Officer Mathew was insufficiently experienced in night flying on instruments, or that his flight instruments had failed, or one of his engines. It was clear, however, that he had lost control.

In 1997 Mr Frederick Kenworthy, of Hillcliff farm, was constructing field drains when he unearthed a significant amount of debris. Among it was part of the battledress blouse belonging to Sergeant Frederick Doe, with a pocket containing a wallet.

In this, Sergeant Doe had been carrying his Pay and Service Book, and his Form 1250 Identity Booklet. His green identity disc, stowed inside his wallet, also survived (both green and red discs should have been worn around the neck). There was, too, a booklet detailing fault-finding procedures on the main radio transmitter-receiver of the day, the T1145/R1155 ('Don't think it doesn't matter not to know your set inside out – the lives of your fellow crew members depend on your knowledge and skill … don't get flustered …').

There were coupons, entitling him to buy chocolate and soap, also cigarettes, variously priced at both sixpence halfpenny for twenty and ninepence for twenty. And there were Wartime-Issue banknotes, five of the blue one-pound notes, and a mauve ten-shilling note: a tidy sum! Sergeant Doe's pay-book shows that until a short while before he had been receiving substantive pay of just three shillings and sixpence a day. This was swelled by War Pay at sixpence a day, giving him a balance of four shillings a day, of which one shilling was being voluntarily deducted. Since gaining his WOp/AG brevet and sergeant's rank, however, he had been getting nine shillings a day.

There was a photograph of him in his flying clothing, although this had deteriorated, leaving only a ghostly image. And there was a specimen will form, left blank, as was the F295 Leave Pass carried in his wallet, clearly to be used on opportunity. And perhaps most poignant of all, for comfort, his knotted necktie had been slipped over his head and stowed.

In 2006, the Ministry of Defence were unable to contact Sergeant Doe's family; accordingly his effects were lodged with the Norfolk and Suffolk Aviation Museum at Flixton.

Visiting the Site
The backfilled crater has left a slight depression. A public footpath leaves the B5023 on the bridge out of Idridgehay at SK 29362 47900 and after 460 yards leads abeam the crater site, itself on private farmland.

10

Matlock

14 AIRSPEED OXFORD Mk 1 BG197
Starkholmes, above Matlock Bath

SK 30182 58639 (153 m)
Unit and Station: No. 14 (Pilots) Advanced Flying Unit, RAF Ossington, north-west of
  Newark, No. 21 Group, Flying Training Command
Date: 3 March 1943
Crew: pilot, killed:
Pupil pilot Sergeant George Howard McIlraith, Royal New Zealand Air Force

When he got airborne on a three-leg, night navigation sortie, Sergeant George McIlraith was well into his ten-and-a-half week course of advanced pilot training and had logged 30 of his 200 hours on Oxfords. He would have been flying over a diligently blacked-out land, but when he wanted to fix his position he descended from the safe altitude laid down for the exercise.

Certainly he was on track for his base at RAF Ossington, then just twenty-nine miles – eleven minutes – distant. However, he failed to take into account the terrain, for having overflown the western rim of the Matlock Gorge, he then flew directly into its eastern rim above the village of Starkholmes.

The court of inquiry could only record that having become lost, Sergeant McIlraith had then failed to maintain a safe height.

George Maskery, aged seven at the time, found the aircraft's signal pistol and surrendered it to the RAF salvage team. His brother Ben, however, aged six, was clearly more entrepreneurial, for having fashioned rings from the fragmented perspex windscreens, he disposed of them for unspecified gain through barter with the local maidens.

Visiting the Site
The crash site lies below Starkholmes' White Tor Road, the upper – and lesser – of the two roads serving the village, but is on such a steep and slippery slope that even getting a GPS fix may prove difficult. Further, the slope has long been used by fly-tippers, notwithstanding which scraps of debris were still to be found in 2012. To access, leave White Tor Road at SK 30228 58644.

15 DE HAVILLAND MOSQUITO Mk 2 HJ929 (SEE FIGS 33–35)
Balk Wood, Dethick, south-east of Matlock

SK 32132 58811 (176 m)
Unit and Station: No. 410 (Cougar) Squadron, Royal Canadian Air Force, RAF Coleby
   Grange, south of Lincoln, No. 12 Group, Fighter Command
Date: 16 August 1943
Crew: two, parachuted, injured
Warrant Officer A. F. Thomas, pilot
Sergeant K. J. Spargo, navigator, broken leg

The Mosquito, successful as it was, was inherently prone to the aerodynamic problem known as 'flutter', a phenomenon manifested when structures are set flexing beyond the limit to which they can be damped – as with bridges when boy scouts don't break step on crossing them ... Modifications helped, but despite limitations embodied in *Pilot's Notes*, the problem remained.

Warrant Officer Thomas, flying Mosquito HJ929, was engaged in camera-gun attacks against a target aircraft. Only this was an exercise in which competitiveness could lead crews to push performance boundaries: precisely the sort of thing that could induce flutter …

Certainly, in the course of one of his attacks Warrant Officer Thomas experienced judder when he entered a left turn. Then, on a subsequent left turn the judder became so violent that it actually flicked the aircraft inverted. Warrant Officer Thomas managed to recover from the ensuing dive, only to have the aircraft fall into a rapidly-rotating and uncontrollable spiral to the right.

Assessing the situation, Warrant Officer Thomas jettisoned the canopy and ordered his navigator, Sergeant Spargo, to abandon the aircraft. As the canopy went, however, so the aircraft reared up, the increased acceleration forcing the blood from his head, causing him to black out and then lose consciousness. Even so, he was aware of two distinct shocks as both the canopy and Sergeant Spargo came into contact with the tailplane. But possibly this altered the flight forces, for he gradually came to, managing to leave the now climbing aircraft himself at 6,000 feet and making a successful parachute descent. Sergeant Spargo, he then found, had also survived, despite suffering a broken leg. For its part, the aircraft had fallen off the top of its climb to impact into Balk Wood at Dethick.

After much deliberation, the court of inquiry submitted that its only sure finding could be that loss of control had led to the abandonment and, therefore, to the destruction of the aircraft.

Mr John Else, of Lea Moor Farm, was a schoolboy at the time. 'When we reached the aeroplane,' he recalled, 'all they had guarding it were police and Home Guard. So we had no problem looking over it and bringing away bullets and the like …' Indeed, such ammunition scavenging led to the police touring the area, seeking its return.

Civil engineer Mr David Radford, of Lea, was a keen aircraft crash-site excavator in the 1960s and 1970s. 'Most of the wreckage,' he explained, 'including the engines, was retrieved by the RAF, while an enthusiast group from Rolls-Royce took away a lot more.' He went on, 'Then, in 1980, having obtained a licence from the Ministry, I got permission to dig from the owner, the redoubtable Mrs Fanny Collier. I spent weeks pumping water away – using my lawnmower motor – as I excavated the crater, recovering propeller components and various gearings. Finally,' Mr Radford concluded, 'I backfilled the site, and restored the driveway.'

Visiting the Site

The impact crater is in strictly-private woodland, beneath a drive. Odd fragments of debris do emerge thereabouts, however, and while an honest approach might gain permission to visit, *soi-disant* 'researcher ID' is not welcome.

11

Stoke

16 VICKERS WELLINGTON Mᴋ 1C R1538 (SEE FIGS 36–37)
Captain's Barn Farm, Cellarhead, near Stoke

SJ 95122 45944 (239 m) initial impact point, tailplane detached
SJ 95095 45820 (228 m) terminal impact point of wings and fuselage
SJ 95146 45880 (245 m) memorial
Unit and Station: No. 28 Operational Training Unit, RAF Wymeswold, north-east of
   Loughborough, No. 93 Group, Bomber Command
Date: 30 January 1943
Crew: five, two killed, two seriously injured, one slightly injured
Sergeant C. A. Reynolds, RAF, pilot, injured
Sergeant Bull, RAF Volunteer Reserve, second pilot, air experience, injured
Flight Sergeant Thomas Butterley, RAFVR, observer, killed
Sergeant Alan Priest, RAFVR, air bomber, killed
Flight Sergeant Royston R. Clarke, RAFVR, wireless operator/air gunner

The final exercise of the operational training unit course at Wymeswold was meant to simulate an operational sortie, routing participating crews to Scotland and back to get a representative length.

Most crews landed after some six hours forty-five minutes, but a full seven and a quarter hours after take-off Sergeant C. A. Reynolds and his trainee crew crashed at Captain's Barn Farm, near Cellarhead, forty miles from Wymeswold. Flight Sergeant Thomas Butterley, the observer, and air bomber Sergeant Alan Priest were killed; the pilots, Sergeants Reynolds and Bull, were seriously injured. Sergeant Royston Clarke, however, manning the wireless-operator's position directly behind the captain, was only slightly injured and raised the alarm.

The court of inquiry acknowledged the heavy demands made upon the crew, submitting, 'Inexperienced crew encountered bad weather at the conclusion of a long and tiring flight.'

As Mr Herbert Myatt, then a boy living at nearby Hulme, remembered, 'My uncle Herbert, who farmed Captain's Bar, was woken at just gone two in the morning by a distressed airman knocking at his door.' This, it transpired, was Flight Sergeant Clarke.

Having visited the site the next day, Mr Myatt recalled, 'The fuselage, wings and engines were just inside the hedged banking of the Twelve Acre Field, where they'd made three great holes. Beyond that, debris ran back a hundred yards or so towards Moorville Hall, to where the tail lay, on the crest, still facing Captain's Barn. The turret hadn't a shard of perspex left.'

The site was swiftly cleared. As Mr Myatt recalled, 'They tried to get their Bedford Queen Marys into the field but couldn't make it. So all the wreckage had to be taken by cart to the edge of the main drive and collected from there.'

Mr Myatt went on to farm Captain's Barn himself, and in September 1995, in conjunction with Mr John Butterley, the son of the navigator of R1538, and its erstwhile air gunner, Flight Sergeant Royston Clarke, erected a memorial to the crew. By intent, to ensure its permanence when so many fields were being enlarged, this was not positioned where the crew members died but at the corner of the wood abutting the field. [Indeed, an application to quarry in the adjoining field was made, but refused in 2006.]

In 1993, author Marshall Boylan was able to confer with survivor Flight Sergeant Clarke, learning that, in view of the low fuel state, an on-board decision had been made to divert to RAF Ashbourne, a crew-derived input which allows a reconstruction to be made of the last stages of the ill-starred flight.

Although engaged in a final, pre-operational exercise with radio silence imposed, the participating crews were permitted to transmit for a homing as their navigators' plots indicated that it was time to begin their descents to Wymeswold, particularly in view of the poor weather. When Flight Sergeant Butterley plotted their received bearing, however, it showed that they were well west of track, certainly closer to Ashbourne than Wymeswold. A hurried consultation then followed, with uneasy reference to the fuel gauges, and the politic decision was made to put down at Ashbourne.

The bearing, though, left them unaware that they were further south too than they thought, also that the terrain they were descending into through rain and thick cloud rose to 750 feet above sea level. In contrast, Wymeswold, to which their altimeter was set, was at only 270 feet above sea level. When they struck, therefore, their altimeter would still have been reading some five hundred feet!

As it happened, R1538 was not the only exercise aircraft to fall into the blind-descent trap, for thirty minutes earlier the crew of Wellington R1011, believing they were far further south than they were, had impacted on Bleaklow while making a similar letdown. The Air Officer Commanding, faced with both crash reports, and with yet more prospective operational aircrew lost through blind descents being made through cloud, could only blankly recommend, 'No further action.'

Visiting the Site

A drive now leads from the farmhouse over what were formerly fields. But continuous farm activity and several excavations have made debris very rare, though the concrete memorial remains, modestly fashioned and dedicated without ostentation.

12
Cellarhead

17 HANDLEY PAGE HALIFAX Mk 2 BB320 (SEE FIGS 38–39)
Blakeley Lane Farm (effectively, New Farm), Cellarhead, Staffordshire

SJ 97409 47408 (258 m)
Unit and Station: No. 1662 Heavy Conversion Unit, RAF Blyton north-east of Gainsborough,
    No. 1 Group, Bomber Command
Date: 7 February 1944
Crew: six, all killed
Pilot Officer Ernest Charles David Richards, RAF Volunteer Reserve, pilot
Pilot Officer Hubert Lloyd Kerr, Royal Canadian Air Force, navigator
Sergeant Kenneth Murray, RAFVR, navigator
Sergeant Albert John Denny, RAFVR, flight engineer
Sergeant William Desmond Joshua, RAFVR, wireless operator/air gunner
Sergeant Herbert John Couling, RAFVR, air gunner

Flying Officer Ernest Richards and his trainee crew had been airborne in Halifax BB320 for some forty-five minutes on a night cross-country exercise when he entered cloud. His aircraft suffered a severe ice build up and after two engines failed, it spun into the ground and burst into flames. All on board died, although the rear gunner, Sergeant Herbert Couling, was thrown clear.

Flying Officer Richards had logged 800 hours total flying but just fifteen on the Halifax, and just three on the type at night. His pre-flight briefing had been to 'fly around clouds,' but it might be conjectured that he had hoped to pass swiftly through a layer which, in the ineluctable way of cloud, then proved more substantial than he had thought.

Investigators found that two of the engines had not been providing power on impact. Even so, they also considered possible icing-up of the flying controls. On balance, however, they concluded that carburettor icing had caused a double engine failure and that the pilot, inexperienced on type, had been unable to contain the resulting asymmetric condition on instruments, and at night, and had lost control, stalling, then spinning into the ground.

Not without reluctance, Mr Joe Whilock, of Wallmires Farm, Cellarhead, spoke of his own involvement. 'We saw that the rear gunner had been thrown clear. So we ran to drag him to safety. But the moment we touched him we could see that he was dead. Then the heat got to us, for the front of the plane was well alight. And there was ammunition banging away all over the place and zipping past. So we had to leave him there. Afterwards he was taken up to Blakeley Lane Farm on a cart ...'

When pressed, Mr Whilock only grudgingly conceded that he had been well aware that the aircraft could have exploded at any instant. 'But the rear of the plane,' he insisted, 'wasn't on fire.'

It is to be regretted that the RAF were never made aware of his gallantry!

Visiting the Site

The crash site, on strictly private ground, normally shows nothing but a spongy depression at the terminal point, the result of an enthusiast excavation.

13

Cheadle

18 ARMSTRONG WHITWORTH WHITLEY Mк 5 LA765 (see fig 40)
Dilhorne, Cheadle

SJ 97256 44678 (215 m) The initial impact point, a pond.
SJ 97303 44868 (200 m) Terminal site, a gully.
Unit and Station: No. 81 Operational Training Unit, RAF Ashbourne, No. 38 Group, Allied
   Expeditionary Air Forces Command (AEAF)
Date: 31 January 1944
Crew: five, four killed, one survived, injured:
Sergeant Ian Leslie Wilkinson, pilot
Flying Officer John Frederick Cusworth, navigator
Sergeant George Victor Bourne, bomb aimer
Flight Sergeant A. H. Robinson, wireless operator
Flight Sergeant T. H. Weightman, air gunner, survived, injured

As the date for the invasion of Europe approached, the Whitleys of No. 81 Operational Training Unit switched from preparing crews for heavy bombers and began training them for the glider-tug role.

Which role Sergeant Ian Wilkinson and his crew had been scheduled to fulfil is not known. But twenty minutes after take-off on a night cross-country flight, their Whitley struck rising ground near Dilhorne, just thirteen miles west of Ashbourne, bounced, turned turtle, and nosed into a gully in flames. Only the rear gunner, Flight Sergeant T. H. Weightman, survived to raise the alarm at the nearby Foxfield Wood colliery.

The survivor's evidence showed that, although unit flying orders dictated that the crew avoid rather than penetrate cloud, the pilot had not only ignored the navigator's advisory to that effect but had flown at near zero on the altimeter.

Accordingly, the court of inquiry's finding was clear: flying orders had been disobeyed, the aircraft having been flown in cloud at well below the safety height.

At that time Mrs Marjorie Mears, née Wheat, was a child living at Whitehurst Farm. The whole area was wooded,' she remembered wistfully, 'not scrub as it is now. And mother was quite happy to let us play there. We'd find bits of metal and nuts and bolts and the like in the water. Once we found a flying glove …'

Visiting the Site
Lay-by parking can be found at Whitehurst, in Whitehurst Lane, at SJ 97484 45224. Following a track (on 202°M) to cross the Foxfield Steam Railway line – with care – and then Foxfield Wood leads to the gully site in 450 yards. In 2012 it was still possible to find blue corrosion and the occasional shard of metal.

19 DE HAVILLAND DH112 Mk 1 VENOM WK390 (see figs 41–42)
Handley Bank, Caverswall

SJ 95189 43844 (219 m)
Operator: Ministry of Supply
Date: 22 February 1954
Crew: pilot, killed
Mr Kenneth Burton Forbes, Fairey Aviation Company test pilot

Mr Kenneth Burton Forbes, a Fairey Aviation test pilot working from Manchester's Ringway aerodrome, was killed when he encountered a problem that led to his aircraft crashing into a field at Cocking Farm. The machine exploded on impact, creating a sizeable crater and spreading debris for nearly a mile. The location of parachute fragments showed that no attempt had been made to evacuate.

With little to go on, witness evidence played a large part in the investigation, Mr Natham Atkinson, of Cookshill, testifying, 'The plane came out of the clouds in a power dive only about a hundred yards from the earth, and crashed.'

The cause was never established. But due tribute was paid by Mr Marshall, the North Staffordshire coroner, who observed, 'This is a very brave occupation – this test pilot business.'

Visiting the Site
Access is from Handley Banks (Lane), north-easterly from Caverswall. On private farmland, the very large crater has been backfilled, leaving only a minor depression.

20 REPUBLIC P-47D THUNDERBOLT 42-22491
Riverside, Upper Tean, Staffordshire

SK 00786 39584 (133m)
Unit and Station: 551st Fighter Training Squadron, 495th Fighter Training Group, United States
    Eighth Army Air Force, AAF342 (RAF Atcham), Shrewsbury
Date: 14 July 1944
Crew: pilot, killed
Second Lieutenant Donald M. Pfaff, USAAF

The function of the 495th Fighter Training Group was to accustom American fighter pilots to conditions in the European theatre. On 14 July 1944, however, Second Lieutenant Donald Pfaff encountered a problem while dog-fighting and, unable to maintain control, dived into a row of cottages at Riverside, in Upper Team. Second Lieutenant Pfaff was killed but there were no casualties on the ground.

Mrs Evelyn Williams, of Upper Tean, 102 in 2010, demonstrated her clear recall of that day. 'My husband, Les,' she said, 'had just gone off to work on the night shift when I heard this plane coming. Then there was this most enormous crash, and everything seemed to come down. I put my hands on my head, and just began to scream.'

'At that time,' Mrs Williams continued, 'there were four cottages here. Where the plane hit, next to us, there was old Mr Hill, and beside him, Mr and Mrs Richard Wood, a young couple. She'd gone off to the pictures. Their oldest, Brian, was in the kitchen, and Ian was in his cot upstairs, so their dad had nipped out to pick up an accumulator for the wireless. However, two men clambered in and rescued them, and everyone else was all right.'

Mrs Williams smiled. 'I simply stayed where I was. So when a policeman appeared he was so shocked to find me that he yelled, "Mrs Williams, what are you still bloody doing here?"– he actually swore! For there was petrol everywhere and bullets. And when they took me outside all the chimney pots had gone. As it turned out, it was eighteen months before the Americans paid the landlord and he got the properties done up. But then the end cottage kept being hit by road traffic. Until one day, when the lady was on the toilet, a lorry lost control and took away all the other rooms. So that cottage was demolished for safety.'

Visiting the Site

There is adequate opportunity parking near Riverside Road, in Upper Tean, where a plaque recording the tragedy has been placed on the front wall of the surviving cottages.

14

Waterhouses

21 AIRSPEED OXFORD Mk 1 R6271 (SEE FIGS 43–46)
Waterhouses, Hamps Valley, The Manifold Way

SK 09328 50128 (252 m)

Unit and Station: No. 42 Operational Training Unit, RAF Ashbourne, No. 38 Group, Army
    Co-operation Command

Date: 21 May 1943

Crew: pilot and two air-experience passengers, all killed

Pilot Officer Archibald Douglas Vincent Forsyth, Royal New Zealand Air Force, pilot

Corporal Harry Garnet Sylvester, RAF Volunteer Reserve

Leading Aircraftman Harry Charles Halestrap, RAF Volunteer Reserve

Pilot Officer Archibald Forsyth, a New Zealander, had been authorised to carry out an air test and had agreed to take along two airmen for the ride. Shortly after take-off, however, his aircraft was seen flying at very low level down the Hamps Valley – the Manifold Way. At Waterhouses he pulled up to clear the valley but struck the power cables strung from bank to bank, nosed into the hillside and exploded in flames. There were no survivors.

The air test did not call for low flying, accordingly the court of inquiry found that the pilot had disobeyed regulations and in so doing destroyed his aircraft and killed himself and his passengers. Additionally, they observed, 'Non ops' – not an operational sortie – so branding the crash a total squandering of life and materiel.

Mr Ray Sutton, then a boy living at Pitchings Farm, just up the Hamps Valley, saw the last moments of the fateful flight.

'Aircraft frequently used to low fly down the valley,' he said, 'but I was looking down on this one! There's a long, straight stretch as far as the farm, but at that point most low flyers pulled up to the right. This one, though, stayed low. But just moments later there was this explosion, then a plume of black smoke.' He paused. 'Dad and I ran down the valley. And even before we came to the west-bank pylon we began to find pieces of plywood: they must have sprung back, like from a bow. We could see that the top cable hadn't been touched, but both the others had carried away. Indeed, one had caught on his right-hand engine, swinging him into the left bank.'

He shook his head. 'We scrambled across the river bed and found it had come down just below a drystone wall about twenty feet above us. But it wasn't an aircraft, just a ball of fire ...'

Visiting the Site
Parking is available by the A523 at Waterhouses at SK 09016 50172. Having taken the Manifold Way path, a gate opens off to the right at SK 09178 50162. Angling across the meadows, the site is on the very steep and slippery far bank of the normally dry river. In 2012 it was still possible to find debris shards beneath the leaf mould. And upstream, the power cables continued to span the gorge.

15
Ashbourne

22 ARMSTRONG WHITWORTH ALBEMARLE P1554 (SEE FIGS 47–49)
The Mount, North Avenue, Ashbourne

SK 17919 46981 (156 m)
Unit and Station: No. 42 Operational Training Unit, RAF Ashbourne, No. 38 Group, Air Defence of Great Britain Command.
Date: 18 December 1944
Crew: four, plus a supernumerary, one killed, remainder injured
Flight Lieutenant Ken Turner, pilot, eventually lost an eye
Pilot Officer Arthur Bunting, navigator, killed
Sergeant Derek Coleman, air gunner, slightly injured
Sergeant Dave Rudge, wireless operator, slightly injured
Flying Officer Tommy Wardlaw, Royal Canadian Air Force, navigator/bomb aimer, supernumerary, severe head injury

Flight Lieutenant Ken Turner and his trainee crew had been engaged in several days of intensive navigation training when he made his 0400 hours approach to Ashbourne's south-easterly runway (in modern terms, Runway 14). The town itself, though, is built in a basin, and as he crossed its northern rim he sank too low, his wheels clipping a tree and bringing his nose down so that he crashed into the pitched roof of The Mount on North Avenue.

None of the resident Wardlow family was hurt although eight bedrooms were swept away and one female domestic was temporarily trapped in her room. Of the crew, however, Pilot Officer Arthur Bunting, the navigator, was thrown clear and killed, while pilot Flight Lieutenant Turner suffered severe facial lacerations that cost him an eye. Supernumerary Flying Officer Tommy Wardlow suffered severe head injuries that were to hospitalise him for some time but the other two crew members emerged virtually unscathed.

The aircraft ended up resting tail high on the structure and nose down into the garden, venting enormous quantities of fuel. Despite this, one well-meaning rescuer, aware of the rear-gunner calling, 'Get me the hell out of here', sought to bring an ignited blowlamp into use only to have a petrol- and oil-soaked Flying Officer Tommy Wardlow earnestly – but succinctly – request him to both desist and depart ...

The crew members were quickly removed to hospital, leaving salvage workers to load the wreckage onto Queen Mary trailers. Naturally, the crash was the talk of Ashbourne, but the newspapers were muzzled by the wartime embargo on publishing anything that might give 'comfort to the enemy'.

Returning to Ashbourne from Canada in 1993, former Flying Officer Wardlow filled in some of the background for Mr Stewart Wilson, an early site visitor. 'I was detached to the RAF,' Mr Wardlow explained, 'to develop tactical map-reading skills for dropping supplies to partisans and forward-troop positions. It had meant a long and tiring series of flights, and that morning we were unashamedly bushed.'

He went on, 'Being so underpowered, the Albemarle was a disaster, but it was standard practice for crew members to vacate the bomb-aimer's position for landing. On this occasion, though, Arthur stayed in the nose ...'

Preparing for the meeting, Mr Wilson had discovered that of the two sergeants, one had died in a car accident, and one of illness, but at least he had been able to locate former Flight Lieutenant Turner in Hereford and so re-unite him with his Canadian supernumerary.

Visiting the Site

In the late 1940s the Bagshaws, faced with wartime shortages when seeking to rebuild, settled for fewer upper rooms and a flat roof with a classically Palladian parapet. The Mount, therefore, remains an elegant – and very private – house.

23 VICKERS WELLINGTON T.10 LP397 (SEE FIGS 50–51)
Church Mayfield, Ashbourne

SK 15449 44950 (115 m)
Unit and Station: No. 28 Operational Training Unit, RAF Wymeswold, north-east of
   Loughborough, No. 93 Group, Bomber Command.
Date: 13 June 1944
Crew: six, all killed
Flying Officer Joseph Starr, RAF, pilot
Flying Officer George David Wills Buchanan, Royal Canadian Air Force, navigator
Sergeant William Corley Davis, RCAF, bomb aimer
Sergeant William George Paterson, RAF Volunteer Reserve, wireless operator/air gunner

Sergeant Richard John Taylor, RCAF, air gunner
Sergeant James Joseph Ursan Stevens, RCAF, air gunner

Flying Officer Joseph Starr, a pilot of some 1,500 hours experience, had been airborne with his trainee crew for just twenty-five minutes when they inadvertently penetrated a highly active storm cell embedded in a concealing stratiform cloud layer. Not long afterwards, his Wellington crashed at Church Mayfield. There were no survivors.

The court of inquiry reasoned that, as the aircraft had impacted at high speed, and as there was no evidence of structural failure before the crash, the operating pilot had been caught out by the violence of the storm and, unable to settle to instruments, had lost control.

Mr Geoff Allen, of Manor Farm, a lad of five at the time, described the final moments of the flight.

'The day had gone very black and gloomy,' he said, 'and I was sheltering in the barn door by the road when this aeroplane suddenly appeared, then disappeared behind the church. Then there was an explosion, and moments later all this black smoke came up.'

Mrs Janet Bayliss (née Grimshaw) remembered, 'We lived in Clifton, just a mile or so off. My father, Ellis Grimshaw, had been playing tennis with a friend, Flight Lieutenant George Salski, a Polish pilot. We were sheltering from a thunderstorm when this aeroplane came over, not roof-top low, but far lower than most. George Salski cried out, "That aircraft's in trouble, Ellis, come on!" So just moments later, when the explosion came, he and Daddy had already grabbed their bicycles. Daddy plonked me on the old crossbar seat, forgetting that I was ten, and had a bike of my own. We took the short cut by the ginnel but when we got to the church RAF men stopped Daddy, although he was head of the ARP, but let George in.'

The memory was equally vivid for Mr Patrick Smith, then aged eight. 'It was about half-past three when the explosion rocked the school and we all rushed out. There's a large field beyond the church, and then a small pasture, and that's where the aircraft had crashed. There was wreckage everywhere, sprayed towards Middle Mayfield. Ammunition was exploding, there were flames – and there were Horlicks tablets wherever you looked [in-flight energy rations]. And there was a sock, hanging from a tree, and not empty …' He paused. 'There weren't many sentries, so we all took souvenirs. Only, after being told that the RAF were going to search everyone's houses, we threw everything in the river, belted ammunition, the lot.'

In 1995, when the local heritage society of Church Mayfield decided to re-institute the custom of well-dressing which had lapsed a hundred years before, the theme at what is now known as the Peace Well included the ill-fated Wellington. A 2010 initiative has seen a permanent memorial placed in the churchyard (SK 15372 44793).

Visiting the Site
The terminal site is reached by following a footpath for some 260 yards beyond the churchyard. Passing through a kissing gate and turning right along the hedgerow leads to the impact crater, now merely a depression.

24 ARMSTRONG WHITWORTH WHITLEY MK 5 Z9189
Edlaston, Ashbourne

SK 17751 42857 (150 m)
Unit and Station: No. 42 Operational Training Unit and Station (OTU), RAF Ashbourne, No. 70 Group, Air Defence Great Britain Command (Fighter Command).

Date: 27 July 1943
Crew: five, all killed
Flight Sergeant John Alfred Watkins, OTU staff pilot
Flying Officer Ian Bert Mann, trainee pilot
Warrant Officer Ian Wallace-Cox, navigator/bomb aimer
Sergeant Albert John Shorter, wireless operator/air gunner
Sergeant Kenneth Alfred Gooding, air gunner

Later models of Whitley were invariably powered by Merlin engines whose safety features included two 'flame traps': devices designed to reduce the risk of backfires igniting the highly volatile mixture of compressed fuel and air exposed when the inlet valve opened. However, just after Whitley Z9189 had become airborne from RAF Darley Moor, a satellite of RAF Ashbourne, a flame trap failed, taking power from the left engine. With the trainee pilot unable to contain the asymmetric effect, the machine struck the tops of two trees and, scraping past Edlaston Hall, crashed into a field beyond, burning out and killing all the crew.

'It was nearly midnight,' Mr Albert Taylor, of Wyaston, remembered, 'and I'd just left the pub. It should have been blackout but you could read a paper by the firelight. It burnt a fifty-yard ring into the field. But it's the Sunday-dinner smell that I recall …'

Visiting the Site
In 2012 sketchy surface evidence of the crash remained only feet beyond the gate off very narrow Edlaston Lane. Safe roadside parking can be found just a little further up the lane.

16

Muggington

25 ARMSTRONG WHITWORTH WHITLEY Mk 5 BD230 (SEE FIG 52)
Muggington

SK 29523 43980 (167 m)
Unit and Station: No. 42 Operational Training Unit, RAF Ashbourne, No. 38 (Airborne Force)
   Group, Allied Expeditionary Air Force
Date: 24 July 1944
Crew: five, all killed
Sergeant John William Edward Cooper, pilot
Sergeant Henry Cowan, navigator
Sergeant William Brooksbank Smith, bomb aimer
Sergeant William Clifford Norcross, wireless operator
Sergeant Maurice Mitchell Lyon, air gunner

Returning to RAF Ashbourne after a three-and-a-half-hour night flight, Sergeant John Cooper positioned himself at 1,000 feet and called for permission to join the circuit for landing. Having been cleared, he established himself on the downwind leg only for his Whitley to dive near-vertically into the ground, exploding in flames, and killing all on board.

The court of inquiry ruled out disorientation while on instruments, seeing that a visual positioning had already been accomplished. Then, finding no evidence of an engine failure, they speculated that Sergeant Cooper might have collapsed over the controls, so initiating the fatal dive. One area not investigated, seemingly, was that of a too-spirited pull around onto the downwind leg, which could well have led to a stall.

It is axiomatic in air-accident investigations that some witnesses will report any crashed aircraft as having been on fire before impact, and this has certainly been the case here. The RAF investigators, on the other hand, having investigated the accounts that came to their notice, discounted them, eventually submitting that some unknown cause had led to the loss of control.

In this instance, however, it is just possible that an engine may, indeed, have caught fire, so distracting the pilot that he lost control. Farmer George Yates, then manning Observer Corps Station L3 at Hulland, seeing the aircraft coming from the Ashbourne direction, reported to the Derby central control that it had an engine on fire, that it was descending, and just moments later, that it had crashed, lighting up his horizon. Another witness, John Morrison, then sixteen, of Hollyburn Cottages, in Weston Underwood, maintains, 'It was engulfed in flames. Well alight all down one side.' He, though, was not interviewed.

It could well be, of course, as the investigators would have known, that such observers had mistaken for an engine fire the yards-long exhaust flare given off as a piston engine is powered up to level out after a descent: a well-known cause of alarm to passengers and rear-crew alike!

The aircraft embedded itself in a deep crater, the backfilled site being marked by a permanent memorial which commemorates, too, the three crew members who were left interred.

Visiting the Site
The most convenient route to the site is via Leasow Farm, although the public footpath skirting the site offers access – and a pleasant short walk – from the north. Debris which emerges is often laid on the monument.

17
Sudbury

26 REPUBLIC P-47C REPUBLIC THUNDERBOLT 41-6259 (SEE FIG 53)
Sudbury Coppice, Sudbury

SK 15617 35518 (105 m)
Unit and Station: United States Eighth Army Air Force, 27th Ferry Group, 311th Ferrying
   Squadron, AAF329 (RAF Halesworth), south-west of Lowestoft.
Date: 19 January 1944
Crew: pilot, killed
Second Lieutenant Dennis J. Robinson, USAAF

Second Lieutenant Dennis Robinson was detailed to fly as wing-man of a two-ship ferry from the Lowestoft area to RAF Maghaberry, a satellite of RAF Long Kesh, in Northern Ireland. That he had just four hundred hours total and had done no instrument flying in the previous six months says much about the dispatching authority who sent him off on a *visual* flight clearance in conditions of total cloud cover with heavy rain and scud giving poor visibility at any low level!

Maintaining marginal ground contact, the pair had flown for some 140 miles when Second Lieutenant Robinson became unsettled, his aircraft pulling up, then falling away into the overcast, clearly out of control. The leader, unable to determine what had happened to his wingman, eventually set course again, and climbing to 3,500 feet, and flying on instruments, arrived safely at RAF Maghaberry.

Second Lieutenant Robinson's aircraft struck the edge of Sudbury Coppice at 'terrific speed' (American accident report), impacting and finally exploding in a deep crater.

Woodman Mr Frank Gould told his successor, Mr John Brassington, what he found. 'I hurried north-eastwards from where the plane hit the trees towards Six-Lane-Ends, and saw some oil, then a brass plug. Then, less oil and more metal. The crater itself, though, was a sight that shook me up for years to come.'

The investigators recommended that in the future, pilots detailed to ferry 'tactical airplanes be required to practice instrument flying either in Link Trainers [the flight simulator of the day] or hooded airplanes for a minimum period of one hour per week.'

Regarding the fundamental cause, they pulled no punches, attributing 10 per cent to the weather, 20 per cent to the pilot's lack of instrument flying skills, 30 per cent to the evident lapse of mental efficiency occasioned by unpreparedly entering cloud, but a damning 40 per cent to the faulty judgement of the supervisory officers who had authorised and then cleared the ferry.

Visiting the Site

The site remains a private woodland but if permission is sought to visit, then May is recommended, when the coppice erupts in a glorious profusion that befits its local appellation, 'Bluebell Wood'. Tree cover may make obtaining a GPS reading difficult, but some eighty yards beyond the star-junction of woodland paths named Six-Lane Ends, the still sizeable crater, with metal fragments, is just ten yards to the left (south) of the track.

18

Marchington

27 VICKERS WELLINGTON T.10 MF584 (SEE FIGS 54–55)
Marchington, Staffordshire

Associated sites
SK 12565 29850 (80 m) impact site
SK 12270 29700 (80 m) pilot parachuted
SK 11975 29702 (84 m) two crew parachuted
SK 11660 29400 (110 m) one crew parachuted

SK 12000 29180 (80 m) one crew parachuted

Unit and Station: No. 27 Operational Training Unit, RAF Church Broughton, No. 93 Group, Bomber Command

Date: 18 July 1944

Crew: five, all parachuted, one slightly injured:

Flight Sergeant J. S. Walker, Royal Australian Air Force, pilot

The other four crew members are presently unidentified.

Flight Sergeant Walker and his trainee crew were engaged in practice bombing on the Bagot Forest range when a propeller became detached, the resulting vibration jolting the associated engine from its mountings and rendering the aircraft uncontrollable. The Wellington crashed and burnt but all five crew members made successful parachute descents, with just one suffering some slight injury. A technical examination showed that no one, ground- or aircrew, had been derelict in his duty and Flight Sergeant Walker was commended for his captaincy.

Mr Tommy Wood, of Birch Cross Farm, then a lad, saw the crash. 'It was near milking time,' he said. 'The Wellington came from the Abbot's Bromley direction but then dived vertically into the ground with a flash of flame and black smoke.' He paused. 'The only parachute I saw was the pilot's. He landed in Over Leasowe Field, and Mr Longden, of Marchington Hall, took him off to his place.'

Mrs Noreen Appleby, née Glover, of Barns Hill Farm, was eleven at the time. 'One of the airmen,' she remembered, 'landed in the field just outside our house, then began to run towards the road. Father [Bill Glover] stayed with him until he was picked up. And another came down on the far side of our brook.'

Mr John Snow lived at Field House Farm. 'We'd Fire Service and ARP billeted upon us,' he recalled, 'but the driver was off somewhere. So my father drove the fire engine across the fields to the site himself, to find bullets exploding all over the place.'

Visiting the Site

Convenient lay-by parking is available on the B5017 at SK 13085 30159. A footpath from SK 13031 30206 then runs close to the site, 640 yards off, where, despite a major 1992 dig by enthusiasts, surface fragments could still be found beneath a hedge in 2012.

28 VICKERS VARSITY T Mk 1 G-BDFT (EX-WJ897) (see figs 56–59)
Draycott in the Clay, near Marchington, Staffordshire

SK 15103 30064 (226 m) Impact site and memorial

Operator: Leicester Aircraft Preservation Group

Date: 18 August 1984

Occupants: fourteen. Two crew and nine passengers died

Crew and passengers killed:

Mr Henry Trevor Howard, pilot

Wing Commander Ralph William Reid-Buckle

Mr Neil Michael Kinsville (engineer, Orion Airways, ex-British Midland)

Mr Ronald Frederick Arnold; Mr Roy Terence Arnold; Mr Jack Desmond Chapman; Mr Andrew John Piper; Mr Christopher Lawrence Heaps; Mr Michael Lercy Twite; Mr Robert Charles Bailey; Mr John Graham Sperry

Survivors:
Mr Barry Gurr
Mr Roger Somerville
Mr Trevor Follows

The painstakingly restored 1952 Vickers Varsity, resplendent in its red and silver livery, was to be photographed from a Cessna en route to a Liverpool air show. As the pair began the photographic session, however, the Varsity pilot, flying slowly to accommodate the Cessna, declared that his right-hand engine was giving concern. His passengers, and the Cessna's occupants, though, saw backfiring and smoke coming from the left-hand engine.

For photographic purposes the Varsity was asked to drop its undercarriage, but when the pilot found that he was unable to maintain height, he retracted it again, warning that he might have to abort the exercise. Indeed, a little later, he decided to home towards East Midlands Airport, even so declaring that he could maintain height, if with difficulty. Despite this assurance, the Cessna saw him descend from 3,000 feet to 400 feet in a very short time. At that stage the left-hand engine stopped, but was immediately restarted. Then, moments later, the undercarriage was lowered again, only to have the left wing drop and the aircraft roll inverted. Finally, just feet from the ground, it sliced through some power cables before impacting, flipping end over end, and bursting into flames. It came to rest with the tail fin vertical and the rear fuselage in a drainage ditch, only the three passengers in this section surviving. The debris was confined within a mere 250 feet.

One of the survivors, Mr Barry Gurr, would subsequently tell the inquiry, 'There was a banging on the port engine. Then something started to happen with the starboard engine. After which I think we just lost power.'

Farmer's wife Mrs Valerie Langridge, of Moreton Farm, recalled that Sunday morning. 'We were in the kitchen when we saw this aeroplane coming directly towards us, alarmingly low, and with its left engine stopped. But then it began a turn to the left, towards the gliding-club, I suppose. Just the same, we all rushed out of the house. Only to see a great plume of black smoke.'

Mrs Langridge paused. 'Fred, my husband, rushed over to try to help. He found it so traumatic, though, that some time later, when he began to fence off the area, he had to get someone else to finish the job.'

Visiting the Site

Having gained the farmer's permission, limited parking is available on the access track at SK 15149 29781, a gate further along the track leaving a 300-yard field walk to the site. In 2009, twenty-five years on, a modest memorial was placed in the long-since thorn-thicketed enclosure. In 2012 scraps of debris still littered the enclosure, further evidence of the tragedy being provided by the spliced power cables outside the wire.

Vickers Wellington Mk 3 BJ652, Smerrill
See page 37

Below: **27.** Vickers Wellington.

Above: **28.** The crag above which Wellington BJ652 struck, leaving the tailplane teetering.

Right: **29.** The memorial to BJ652 in Youlgreave.

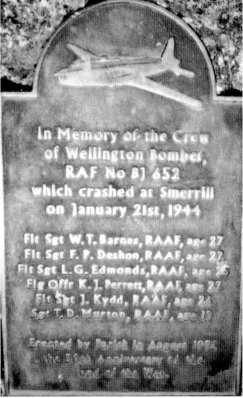

In Memory of the Crew
of Wellington Bomber,
RAF No BJ 652
which crashed at Smerrill
on January 21st, 1944

Flt Sgt W. T. Barnes, RAAF, age 27
Flt Sgt F. P. Deshon, RAAF, age 27
Flt Sgt L. G. Edmonds, RAAF, age 25
Flg Offr K. J. Perrett, RAAF, age 27
Flt Sgt J. Kydd, RAAF, age 24
Sgt T. D. Murton, RAAF, age 19

Erected by Parish in August 1995
the 50th Anniversary of the
End of the War

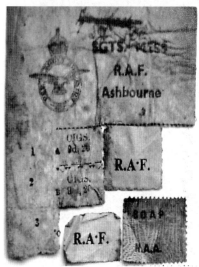

Bristol Blenheim AZ876, Idridgehay
See page 38

Top: **30.** At the crater site in 2011. Inset: Armour plate from the impact site, ploughed up during field-drain laying.

Above right: **31.** Ephemera, mainly coupons, preserved in Sergeant Coe's wallet.

Above left: **32.** An ethereal photograph of Sergeant Coe, preserved in his wallet.

De Havilland Mosquito HJ929, Balk Wood
See page 40

33. De Havilland Mosquito.

34. Surface debris from the woodlands positioned on the impact site of Mosquito HJ929, now once more covered by the drive.

35. (Inset) Debris discovered during authorised excavations by Mr David Radford, of Lea.

IN MEMORY OF
SGT. T. BUTTERLEY 1336746
OBSERVER
SGT A. PRIEST 1312544
BOMB AIMER
KILLED ON THIS SPOT
AT 0215 30/1/43

*Vickers Wellington Mk 1C R1538,
Captain's Barn
See page 41*

Above: **36.** Visitors to the crash site of Wellington R1538 in 1993: survivor ex-flight sergeant Royston Clarke, with Mr Herbert Myatt and aviation author Marshall Boylan.

37. (Inset) The 1995 memorial to R1538.

*Handley Page Halifax Mk 2
BB320, Cellarhead
See page 43*

Left: **38.** At the crash site with a piece of wreckage.

39. (Inset) Mr Joe Whilock, who made a gallant rescue effort when Halifax BB320 crashed.

Armstrong Whitworth Whitley Mk 5 LA765, Dilhorne
See page 44

Top: **40.** The impact site of Whitley LA765.

De Havilland Venom Mk 1 WK390, Cocking Farm
See page 45

Right: **41.** Examining debris from de Havilland Venom WK390.

Above: **42.** The crater site of WK390, with debris. Looking upslope to Intakes Farm.

Airspeed Oxford R6271, Waterhouses
See page 46

43. The power cables Oxford R6271 was flown into.

44. (inset) The terminal impact point of R6271, above the often-dry river bed.

Above left: **45.** The Oxford's P-type compass.

Above right: **46.** A pristine example of a P-type compass.

Armstrong Whitworth Albemarle P1554, The Mount
See page 47

47. Armstrong-Whitworth Albemarle.

48. The Mount, from the rear, flat-roofed, 2012.

49. (Inset) The house as it was in around 1900, showing the extent of the damage caused by the crash.

Vickers Wellington T.10 LP397, Church Mayfield
See page 48

Top: **50.** The terminal impact crater of Wellington LP397, centre, looking across the line of flight towards the church.

51. (Inset) Debris found at the crash site.

Armstrong Whitworth Whitley Mk 5 BD230, Muggington
See page 50

Middle: **52.** The impact site of Whitley BD230, both grave and memorial.

Republic P-47 Thunderbolt, Sudbury Coppice
See page 51

Bottom: **53.** The crater site for Thunderbolt 41-6259, with surface debris, early 2012, looking towards the track through Bluebell Wood.

Vickers Wellington T.10 MF584, Marchington
See page 52

54. The impact site of Wellington MF584. The debris is cached in the hedgerow to the left.

55. (Inset) The debris cache, 2012.

Vickers Varsity T Mk 1 G–BDFT, Draycott
See page 53

56. Vickers Varsity.

57. The scene of the crash of Varsity G-BDFT.

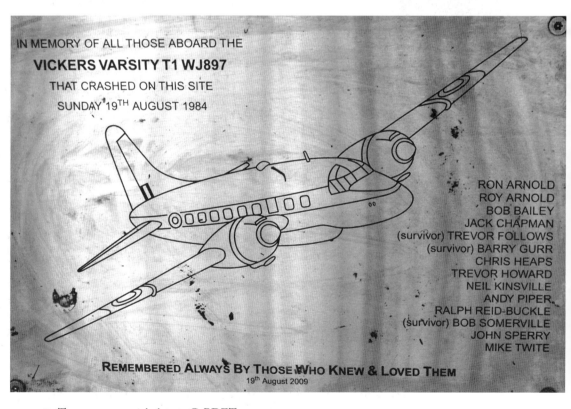

IN MEMORY OF ALL THOSE ABOARD THE

VICKERS VARSITY T1 WJ897

THAT CRASHED ON THIS SITE

SUNDAY 19TH AUGUST 1984

RON ARNOLD
ROY ARNOLD
BOB BAILEY
JACK CHAPMAN
(survivor) TREVOR FOLLOWS
(survivor) BARRY GURR
CHRIS HEAPS
TREVOR HOWARD
NEIL KINSVILLE
ANDY PIPER
RALPH REID-BUCKLE
(survivor) BOB SOMERVILLE
JOHN SPERRY
MIKE TWITE

REMEMBERED ALWAYS BY THOSE WHO KNEW & LOVED THEM
19th August 2009

58. The 2009 memorial plate to G-BDFT.

59. The impact site of G-BDFT, beyond the power cables, long since become a thicket.

PART TWO
SITES WITH NO SURFACE DEBRIS

1

Bosley

29 AIRSPEED OXFORD Mᴋ 1 DF408 (sᴇᴇ ꜰɪɢ 60)
Dawson Farm, Bosley, near Macclesfield

SJ 93163 67270 (378 m) impact site
SJ 93167 67318 (376 m) terminal site
Unit and Station: No. 1531 Beam Approach Training Flight, RAF Cranage, south-west of
    Macclesfield, No. 5 Group, Flying Training Command
Crew: two, one injured
Flying Officer G. C. Smith, Royal Canadian Air Force, instructor, injured
Pupil pilot, unidentified
Date: 15 January 1943

On 15 January 1943, staff instructor Flying Officer Smith, of the Royal Canadian Air Force, was detailed to carry out an instructional sortie of Standard Beam Approaches. Twenty minutes after take-off, his aircraft, flying outside the safe range of the facility, and in cloud, struck a hillside. Flying Officer Smith slightly hurt his foot but both he and his pupil found succour at Dollards Farm, Sutton.

In later years, with improved instrumentation, beam approaches became very straightforward. But in 1943 the system was more rudimentary. Certainly, timing played an essential part.

On flying away from the airfield at 1,000 feet to position for the approach, the pilot would hear the Inner Marker (marking the start of the runway) and would then expect to hear the Outer Marker something like 45 seconds later. If it failed to come up, however, then he should have been on his guard, for to fly any great distance beyond the Outer Marker was to move outside the safety height for the approach.

The board of inquiry duly established that when no Outer-Marker signal was heard – almost certainly because the aircraft had already drifted off the beam – the pupil had been allowed to carry on 'for at least four minutes', flying so far beyond the safe sector that the machine had crashed a full twelve miles from the airfield at some 1,300 feet above sea level, but only 1,100 feet above the elevation of Cranage.

However, the inquiry then submitted that the pupil pilot had made 'an error of judgement in that he failed to hear the signal', compounding this with 'failing to appreciate the lapse of time', a finding upheld by all higher authorities. Yet how strange! For the inquiry advanced as only a supplementary cause, 'the pre-occupation of the pilot instructor when faced with conditions he had not previously encountered': except that, as the pilot instructor, Flying Officer Smith was wholly responsible for the safety of the flight.

Mrs Evelyn Naden, who was brought up on Golden Hill Farm, Bosley, had vivid memories of the crash.

'It was a very misty day,' she recalled, 'and the aeroplane hit near the top of the Sutton Moor ridge, in Dawson Farm's Black Hill Field. It's marshy, with a never-failing spring just below where the plane touched down, so it skidded left and slid on through the drystone wall onto Upton Fold Farm's land. Having got out, the two men followed the wall up through the mist and then down, until they struck the Dollards Farm track. They only just missed the radar station – it was sited rather lower down than the 1947 GPO tower – where there were phones, the airmen being billeted at Dollards and Golden Hill farms.

The aeroplane was on its belly but still so whole that the sentries let us sit in the cockpit. Eventually, though, the RAF chopped it into pieces and my father dragged it down to Upton Fold Farm, then carted it off. It was only a farm track then, but the route was the same: uphill from Upton Fold Farm – past where the GPO tower is now – beside Lingerds Farm, then down past the entrance to Dollards Farm, and finally to the A54, where the RAF had one of their long low-loaders.

Visiting the Site

Having left the A54 at SJ 93826 67201, parking offers along the metalled track towards the GPO tower. Although there is no surface evidence the marshy ground above the spring marks the site. But what a view over the Cheshire Plain! A plain, ironically, that would have presented not the slightest obstacle, had DF804 only been turned back towards Cranage at the proper time.

30 DOUGLAS C-47 SKYTRAIN 41-38608 (SEE FIGS 61–62)
Dawson Farm, Bosley, Macclesfield

SJ 92674 66630 (232 m)
Unit and Station: United States Ninth Army Air Force, No. 363 Tactical Air Command, 333rd
  Photographic Reconnaissance Squadron, Le Culot (Belgium)
Date: 22 December 1944
Occupants: seven, three passengers, four crew, six died
Major Theodore A. Rogers, aircraft captain, survived
First Lieutenant J. E. Barnby, co-pilot
Technical Sergeant W. E. Davis, crew
Technical Sergeant C. P. Ingram, crew
Lieutenant-Colonel R. L. Cardozo, passenger
Lieutenant-Colonel H. R. Payne, passenger
Major David C. R. Steele, passenger, survived only briefly

On 22 December 1944, when Major Theodore Rogers and his crew were dispatched from American Air Force designated airfield AAF590 (RAF Burtonwood), near Liverpool, they carried three senior-officer passengers and a freight load, which included a jeep. The weather was cloudy, with nine-tenths cover, a base of just 800 feet, and a visibility below cloud reduced to 1,100 yards by mist and industrial haze. Not totally unreasonable conditions. However, after flying for just 27 miles their machine struck a tree, crashed into a pasture, and then burnt out, with only the handling pilot, Major Rogers, surviving.

The American accident investigators submitted that Major Rogers had exercised bad judgment in even attempting to maintain contact by flying below cloud, noting too that although he had logged 1,200 hours, with 88 on C-47s, he had very little experience in instrument flying.

Contemporary practice was to set the altimeter to read zero before take off, and to leave it at that setting throughout the flight. Just before impact, therefore, with Burtonwood being a mere 76 feet above sea level, Major Rogers' altimeter would have been indicating almost 1,000 feet, although, having moved over markedly rising terrain, he was now barely skimming the ground.

Yet what mystifies still is why the aircraft crashed where it did. The initial destination was AAF519, RAF Station Grove, near Wantage, in Oxfordshire, the track for which was some 160°T – effectively south-easterly – and crossed the flat, low-lying Cheshire Plain. Yet the aircraft had flown almost 45°, and fifteen miles, off track!

It is conceivable that the pilot had mis-set either his compass or the gyroscopically-controlled directional indicator (basically a slave compass), and so followed a false heading. On the other hand, the track for another frequently-used American station, AAF555, or RAF Shepherd's Grove, north-east of Bury St Edmonds, Suffolk, was 115°T – effectively easterly – and this track passes virtually overhead the crash site. It is at least possible, then, that the track for Shepherd's Grove was laid in, instead of that for Grove.

Mr Alfred Bullock, of Golden Hill Farm, was able to point out the crash site. The plane,' he recalled, 'came down in Swanslake Field, on Dawson Farm. George Naden, who was then the farmer, and his son, Maurice, ran to see what they could do. The plane was an inferno, but they managed to get two men out, although one died shortly afterwards. When I got there I found debris all over the place, with the main portion in a shallow crater. Only there was a burnt body inside, trapped beneath a jeep ...'

And there, Mr Bullock had touched upon one of the drawbacks of the passenger-cum-freight configuration of the day, when cargo was loaded aft of passengers, potentially hazarding them should the lashings break. In more enlightened times – owing much to tragedies like this – when an aircraft had no underfloor hold, freight would always be loaded forward of passengers.

The recognition afforded Mr Naden and thirteen-year-old Maurice gives a special dimension to this air accident, for apart from letters of appreciation from the Chief Constable of Cheshire, by various major- and brigadier-generals of the American Ninth Air Force, by the Air Council, and by Mr Herbert Morrison, MP, they each received the King's Commendation for Brave Conduct, signed by Prime Minister and Lord of the Treasury, Mr Winston S. Churchill, the Commendation entitling them to wear the silver laurel spray symbolising the gallantry award.

Mrs Betty Steele, the mortally injured Major Steele's widow, later corresponded with the Nadens and was able to tell them that the authorities, worried for the pilot's state of mind, initially withheld from him the fact that his passengers and crew had died, and that even so, he had required care for years. They learnt from her, too, that passengers and crew, concerned by the weather on the day, had actually tossed a coin before deciding to go! Then she actually visited the crash site in 1963. And illumining the sixties, in concluding her final letter, she rather sceptically added to her address America's newly introduced 'zip' code [post code], 'which will make the mail go quicker – so they say.'

Mr Tom Johnson and his brother, Alec, moved to Dawson Farm in 1948. 'The plane crashed,' explained Tom, 'in what we now call Bottom Pasture. It came from the direction of Primrose Bank Farm and the stump of the oak it hit stood on the skyline for years.' He indicated the rule-straight farm drive. 'The drive used to twist alongside the gully where the salvage crew tipped much of the wreckage. But enthusiasts from Macclesfield cleared the gully, as well as the site.'

Visiting the Site

The Dawson Farm track leaves the A54 at SJ 92873 66286. Conceivably, permission could be gained to visit the site, which is 220 yards on 208°M from the farm. As Mr Johnson has indicated, however, enthusiasts did a thorough job, so nothing is to be seen.

31 DO-IT-YOURSELF FLYING APPARATUS
Bosley (possibly Flash Bottom Farm, Quarnford)

SK 02300 66000 (390m)
Owner: Mr Arthur Pulson, injured
Date: 1970–80

Mr and Mrs Frank and Margaret Parker, of Quarnford, remembered this aviation initiative. 'Arthur Pulson built his flying machine,' they agreed, 'at Bosley, just before coming here, for while he turned his hand to many things his great passion was for aviation.' What a character! He resided in a hollowed-out rabbit warren to evade National Service, ditto when faced with Poll-Tax fines, and was brought from police custody to dispose of his lethally unsafe dynamite. His inclusion here, though, is as a pilot, even a pioneer aviator. For he attached a bomber propeller to a Volkswagen engine, constructed a supporting frame, and having started the contraption, strapped himself in and released the restraints. The apparatus successfully carried him up above the trees, but it appears he had given no thought to controlling the craft once it was airborne, firmly allying him with many a pioneer would-be flier! As it was, when the fuel lines emptied, he plunged into a bone-breaking elm tree.

Arthur Pulson was one of many Peakland Icarus figures. Not a Daedalus, however, for the very first aviator knew how to control his flight, carefully planned it, did not take-off too near an elm tree, and therefore, reached his destination safely.

2

Congleton

32 MIGNET FLYING FLEA G-ADVU (SEE FIGS 63–64)
Congleton

SJ 80158 65165 (93 m) Davenport, one Congleton crash site
Owners: the Burns family, Congleton
Date: April 1936

A markedly successful Flying Flea was built by Mr Bob Burns and his three sons, Harold, Alan and Robbie, in their Park Street Garage in Congleton. Once Flea G-ADVU was built, Harold became the pilot, continuing to work from inventor Mignet's book. He made his first flight on 13 January 1936 at the Somerford Park Estate, but on his second he turned to avoid a tree and crashed, sustaining a black eye.

A month later, he made two successful flights, but then ran out of fuel and was forced to set-down to the rear of Davenport Methodist Chapel, striking a tree in the process. The editor of the *Congleton Chronicle*, who had chased after the machine, published a doggerel verse:

Flea, fly, flow, flop, we saw it start, and we heard it stop,
Be he alive, or be he dead – he's crashed his 'plane, and bumped his yed.

He also urged Harold to give up after his 'two useful little crashes' but to no avail. Two months later, though, at Meir Aerodrome, after several successful flights, Harold crashed from an estimated 70 feet, escaping with a badly gashed knee.

Mr Ian Burns, of Wincle, Harold's son, explained, 'Despite a few mishaps, Dad had also done a fair amount of flying, from local parks, or from the flat ground below Bosley Cloud. But eventually his mother, Patience, put her foot down. If Dad wanted to continue to fly, she decreed, he should get lessons on a proper machine. Which is what he did. Even before the government banned unmodified Fleas.'

He paused. 'And then, of course, war broke out. Both Alan and Robbie were accepted for the RAF, and flew throughout the war. Dad had his pilot's licence, but couldn't pass the RAF medical. Instead, he joined the Air Transport Auxiliary, flying eighty-two different types. Then, after the war, he flew on for some years with the local flying club.'

Parts of the Flea, Mr Burns confirmed, lingered on for years. But in 1993 a team led by a Mr Ken Fern built, and then exhibited in the family showrooms, a reconstruction of this most celebrated of Fleas.

3

Buxton

33 HEINKEL HE 111
Buxton Area, 'Above Burbage', 17 March 1942

Author Ron Collier recorded that a Heinkel He 111 came down 'above Burbage', and that two members of its crew, *Leutnant* [pilot officer] Frishau and *Hauptmann* [flight lieutenant] Ernst Fraden, were taken into custody by personnel from No. 28 Maintenance Unit of RAF Harpur Hill. The specific details suggest that there is substance to the report. However, extensive inquiries from Burbage to Flash brought nothing to light.

34 JUNKERS JU 88, KG106
Location unspecified, 3 July 1942

Author Ron Collier gave the date, and named crew members Bergman and Majer. He gave no location, however, so this entry is made for posterity.

4
The Roaches

35 VICKERS WELLINGTON Mᴋ 3 Z1744 (ꜱᴇᴇ ꜰɪɢ 65)
Hen Cloud, Upper Hulme

SK 00942 61177 (302 m) impact
SK 00827 61450 (399 m) terminal
Unit and Station: No. 27 Operational Training Unit, RAF Church Broughton, near Uttoxeter,
    satellite of RAF Lichfield, No. 91 Group, Bomber Command
Date: 20 November 1942
Crew: six, five killed, one survived
Sergeant James Robert Barlow, Royal Australian Air Force, pilot
Flying Officer Keith Pettiford, RAAF, staff navigator
Flying Officer James Love, RAAF, navigator
Sergeant William John Baker, RAAF, bomb aimer
Flight Sergeant T. Buckley, RAAF, wireless operator/air gunner
Flight Sergeant Spencer Cheek, RAAF, rear gunner, only survivor

The task of No. 27 Operational Training Unit was to prepare newly-formed crews for their roles on operational squadrons and specifically to acclimatise those from Canada and Australia to European weather conditions. However, when Sergeant James Barlow and his Royal Australian Air Force crew were detailed for a six-and-a-half-hour navigational flight they did not expect a frolicsome American-manned Spitfire to make a series of dummy attacks and take away their trailing aerial.

Not that this should have unduly affected communications, for there was a spare aerial reel, and besides, given reasonable height, the wireless operator should have had no difficulty in making contact on either R/T or W/T utilising the normal-use fixed aerial. Then again, the pilot should have been able to make contact with his short-range, TR9 High-Frequency transmitter-receiver; at worst, this would have enabled him to use the Darky emergency recovery service, which relied upon short-range communications.

However, when the time came for the aircraft to be homed towards base, no such transmissions were received. It has to be assumed, therefore, that Sergeant Barlow decided to ease down through the cloud to get a visual fix. Except that, unknown to those aboard, the aircraft had already overflown Church Broughton by 23 miles and struck the lower slopes of Hen Cloud, 1,300 feet above sea level, only one crew member surviving.

Mr Vic Rider, of Upper Hulme, was an involved witness. 'We saw it narrowly miss the 100-foot chimney of the William Tatton Dye Works so drove round towards the Roaches House Road, where we saw the smoke. I found the rear gunner, Spencer Cheek, and brought him clear of the flames. But there was nothing to be done for the others …'

The court of inquiry found that Sergeant Barlow had blindly 'descended through cloud in order to obtain his bearings when he was lost'. Alongside this, they recommended that a plea be made to the United States' authorities to warn their pilots of the dangers of distracting trainee crews. But overall the sense comes through of the despair felt by those in authority at yet another example of an aircraft being descended blind through cloud.

The sole survivor, Mr Spencer Cheek, also survived the war itself and duly returned to his home in Australia. He then kept in touch with his rescuer, even making a return visit.

Visiting the Site

There is adequate roadside parking alongside The Roaches. The terminal site, best reached from the track leading to the Roaches House, is some 265 yards on a heading of 352°M from the impact site. Fragments may be found beneath the leaf mould in the wood, but this cannot be classed as a site with debris.

36 SUPERMARINE SPITFIRE Mk 2A P7593 (SEE FIGS 66–67)
Windygates Hall Farm, The Roaches

SK 00305 61650 (256 m)
Unit and Station: Headquarters Service Ferry Pools, No. 421 Flight, RAF Kemble, near
    Cirencester
Date: 17 November 1940
Crew: pilot, killed
Flight Sergeant James Beaumont White, RAF Volunteer Reserve

On Sunday 17 November 1940, ferry pilot Flight Sergeant James White was tasked to deliver newly commissioned Spitfire P7593 on the one-hour-twenty-minute, 300-mile flight from Kirkbride, near Carlisle, to RAF West Malling in Kent.

As forecast, there was considerable cloud cover along the route, so having flown for forty minutes – his half-way timing – Flight Sergeant White decided to fix his position. A good plan, for doing so at this point would mean that, having ascertained any track error, he would only need to double that error in the reverse direction to make good his heading for West Malling.

In fact, he had strayed a mere fifteen miles from his direct track. Unfortunately, when he decided to circle down through cloud to determine this, he was over the Ramshaw Rocks and struck a prominence near the celebrated 'Winking Man' phenomenon, his aircraft subsequently gyrating into the ground and burying itself in a pasture.

Traumatic enough, but the investigators found the reality to be more harrowing yet. For witnesses had heard the aircraft circling overhead for a good forty minutes before the crash. Initially mystified, the investigators eventually found that on nosing down Flight Sergeant White had struck some 'trees on rocks', damaging certain control surfaces but also fundamentally undermining the integrity of his aircraft. The control difficulties had left him able to do nothing but circle, until low-level turbulence had caused his starboard wing and tailplane to break away.

Why no distress call was received and why Flight Sergeant White had not taken to his parachute are questions the investigators do not seem to have asked. It is highly probable, however, that his ferry Spitfire had no radio fitted. As for baling out, he would have been only too well aware that, unable to climb for height, he was still in close proximity to the high ground he had struck and that there was precious little chance of his parachute being afforded time to open. It must have seemed to him that his best hope was to wait, burning off fuel, until a gap in the clouds developed and showed what lay below. Except that the unrelenting turbulence forestalled him.

The salvage team left the engine buried, but it was excavated in 1978 and in 2011 was a prized exhibit at Thorpe Camp Aviation Museum, near Tattershall, in Lincolnshire.

Visiting the Site

Although a footpath passes through Windygates Farm, the site itself is on strictly private ground. In late 2011 there was only a slight declivity to mark the tragedy, although debris enough was found – including belt-linked 0.303 inch calibre ammunition – to re-establish the site.

5

Longnor

37 AIRSPEED OXFORD V3626 (SEE FIG 68)
Fawside Edge, Longnor

SK 06759 65163 (360 m)
Unit and Station: No. 12 Flying Training School, No. 21 Group, Flying Training Command,
    RAF Grantham (post-1944, renamed RAF Spitalgate)
Date: 16 November 1941
Crew: pilot, killed
Leading Aircraftman Raymond Henry Wattie Dix, RAFVR, pupil pilot

When pupil pilot Leading Aircraftman Raymond Dix was dispatched from RAF Grantham for 'local flying and circuits', he wandered sixty miles from his base, became lost in bad weather, and flew into Fawside Edge, Derbyshire.

Mrs Nellie Slack, of Fawside Edge Farm, remembered being shocked by the bang. 'We ran out. But it was far too foggy to see anything. Mind you, we didn't know whether to run fast or slow, not knowing whether it was a good aeroplane, or one of *theirs*.'

Mr Walter Limer was also close by. 'We were working down the hill when we heard the engines power up, but almost at once there was this mighty crash. He'd just missed clearing the brow but it didn't burn.'

In the aftermath, the recovery party were billeted in the cow-barn at the adjacent Edgeside Farm, burying and burning what they did not remove.

Visiting the Site

Parking offers near the two farms, but by 2012 only odd scraps of molten and corroded metal could be found, mostly in the gully beyond the impact point.

6

Monyash

38 ENGLISH ELECTRIC CANBERRA B Mκ 6 WT207 (SEE FIG 69)
Monyash

Associated sites:
SK 16155 66133 (263 m) port mainplane
SK 16340 65895 (276 m) starboard mainplane
SK 15005 65376 (329 m) tailplane and rear fuselage
SK 15979 69304 (280 m) front fuselage
SK 14209 69960 (362 m) rocket motor
SK 15197 66508 (271 m) mainwheel
SK 16401 65420 (296 m) pilot parachuted
SK 16740 66740 (288 m) navigator parachuted
Unit and Station: No. 76 Squadron, detached from RAF Wittering, south of Stamford, Bomber
    Command
Date: 9 April 1958
Crew: two, ejected successfully, both slightly injured
Flight Lieutenant J. Peter F. de Salis, pilot, temporary physiological effects
Flying Officer Patrick Lowe, navigator, frostbite

On 9 April 1958 Canberra WT207, engaged in rocket-motor trials, blew up over Monyash, its debris being widely scattered.

Flight Lieutenant Peter de Salis, a graduate of the Empire Test Pilots' School, and his trials navigator, Flying Officer Patrick Lowe, had taken off from RAF Hemswell, near Lincoln, and climbed towards North Wales to begin the rocket-motor trial. At the planned height, they turned onto a north-easterly heading and switched on the rocket motor in their bomb bay.

The unit responded immediately, thrusting the Canberra to as high as 70,310 feet – the world record altitude, set during earlier trials in August 1957 – far beyond its normal achievable ceiling. The trial complete, the motor was switched off, leaving the aircraft to descend to an altitude where its own engines could support it. However, as the descent neared 56,000 feet, the rocket motor was to be restarted in order to use up the residual, highly volatile fuel before landing. Except that when Flight Lieutenant de Salis pressed the starter switch the motor exploded, effectively blowing the Canberra apart. The pair promptly ejected, so setting another world record for the trials, for the highest emergency ejection to date.

Flying Officer Lowe had a trouble-free descent. Having previously removed his gloves, however, he suffered frostbitten hands and, unable to manipulate the parachute risers, landed heavily on his back. He came to earth near the Monyash to Bakewell road, to be picked up by Mr Raymond Brough, of Rake End Farm, and taken to Bakewell Cottage Hospital.

In Flight Lieutenant de Salis's case, though, the small drogue parachute that should have stabilised his ejection seat failed to operate, the seat spinning so violently that the blood flooding into his head made him fear for his sight. And even when his seat separated and his parachute deployed, its cords were so twisted that the subsequent windings and unwindings caused him to vomit. He landed safely, nevertheless, and was succoured by Mr Colin Slater, and by his brother James, who were rolling nearby fields. They took him to One Ash Grange Farm where Mr Frank Slater and his brother, Charlie, were able to supply hot, sweet tea and a telephone.

Examining himself, Flight Lieutenant de Salis found that one forearm was thickened, 'like Popeye's', as his report was to read, and that his reddened eyes were mere slits in his blood-engorged face.

Both pilot and navigator were taken to Chesterfield Hospital and then to RAF Hospital Halton, in Buckinghamshire, for more detailed checks, but neither was kept from flying for long.

The debris, falling from 56,000 feet, had spread widely, not least in Monyash itself, yet, providentially, without causing damage to either life or property.

Cataloguing the larger components, the complete tailplane and rear section of the fuselage came down beyond the copse fringing Summerhill Farm, to the south of Monyash. One wing landed beside the Lathkill Dale path, the other within three hundred yards of it, upslope, at the corner of the field locally known as Friezland. The front fuselage fell into Deep Dale, a mile and a half to the north.

The RAF set up a tented salvage camp at the entrance to Lathkill Dale, a painted notice pronouncing the site to be RAF Monyash! Debris was pooled here, but RAF parties continued to scour the countryside for some weeks, trying to recover part of the rocket motor.

It was Taddington postmistress Mrs Dorothy Cooper who finally found the unaccounted-for component nearly two miles north of Monyash. As Mr Frank Boam, then of Rockfield House Farm, remembered. 'In those days she'd walk the footpaths from Taddington daily to deliver to Hubber Dale.'

So the search ended. RAF Monyash loaded its assorted scrap onto Queen Mary trailers, folded its tents, and departed. And the village regained its serene normality.

Visiting the Site
Sub-surface debris does exist, even by this so popular path. There is, however, no surface debris to be seen at any of the sites, but what an incentive they give to wander the Monyash area, not least to view the companionable two-seater toilet at One Ash Grange Farm!

39 BRISTOL BLENHEIM Mᴋ 1 L6800
Tagg Lane, Monyash

SK 14310 66390 (269 m)
Unit and Station: No. 2 School of Army Co-operation Flying (Operational Training Unit),
    RAF Andover, No. 22 (Army Co-operation) Group with Command Status
Date: 17 November 1940
Crew: pupil pilot, unhurt
Pilot Officer G. F. Kilburn

Trainee Pilot Officer Kilburn had been dispatched on a detail that required him to land away at Desford, west of Leicester, then return to Andover. However, on the outbound leg he became lost due to bad visibility. Aware of the inadvisability of flying blindly on, he decided to make a wheels-up precautionary landing – wheels-up being the configuration recommended for the tail-wheeled aircraft of the day – at what he would find was Monyash, some 46 miles north-west of Desford.

He chose a suitable field, but the unfamiliarity of holding off to touch down without wheels caused him to overshoot and float through some power lines into the next one, his belly-slide being stopped by a drystone wall. Pilot Officer Kilburn was uninjured and the aircraft not that badly damaged.

As Pilot Officer Kilburn had less than one hundred hours' total flying and only two hours solo on type, no disciplinary action was taken.

Mrs Molly Boam, of Monyash, well remembered being taken to the scene by her grandfather. 'The aeroplane,' she recalled, 'was lying in a field of mine called Sammy's Pringle, the one with the dew pond. It had run into the drystone wall separating mine from my mother's field.'

Visiting the Site

No debris from the incident was found, but parking offers alongside the field.

40 WESTLAND LYSANDER V9729 (SEE FIGS 70–72)
Sparklow, south-west of Monyash

SK 11720 65480 (370 m) first contact, Cronkstone Grange Farm Coppice
SK 12285 65902 (375 m) touchdown wall
SK 12590 65900 (364 m) terminal wall
Unit and Station: No. 6 Anti-Aircraft Co-operation Unit, RAF Ringway, detached to RAF
    Sealand, Queensferry, west of Chester, No. 70 Group, RAF Army Co-operation Command
Date: 30 May 1942
Crew: two, no significant injuries
Flight Sergeant Antoni Ilnicki, Polish Air Force under British Command, pilot
Flight Sergeant George Wainwright, RAF Volunteer Reserve, wireless operator

After exercising with a searchlight battery Flight Sergeant Antoni Ilnicki got lost and, running short of fuel, decided to make a precautionary landing. He accomplished a successful touchdown on an unlit and downsloping pasture at Sparklow, but damaged the undercarriage.

Mr and Mrs Cole, then of Cronkstone Lodge and Cronkstone Grange respectively, had first-hand knowledge of the incident. 'It struck our coppice,' Mr Bill Cole remembered, 'then touched down just after the crest, only almost immediately ran through a stone wall. Then it ran on downhill over the rough until it came to a second stone wall, where a wheel broke off, stopping the plane beside a pit, only yards from the road.'

'Otherwise,' Mrs Irene Cole laughed, 'they might have ploughed on into the bar of the Royal Oak. In fact, wary of Germans, the pub people told them to go to our place, knowing my six brothers were there. Anyway, while I gave the airmen a stiff drink and a meal, some of the lads went to the plane and buried the machine-gun ammunition for safety.'

'And just as well,' she continued. 'For when I couldn't get through to the police I called my uncle at RAF Harpur Hill, only to get told off for using a supposedly secret number.' Again she laughed. 'But that was just the start of things. For as nobody came for them that day, my sister walked them to Monyash for the bus and saw them to Bakewell police station. The plane, though, stayed there for nearly a fortnight as the RAF and Poles sorted things out between them, both the investigators and the recovery airmen staying at our place, so that I was forever cooking.'

In the 1980s, author Ron Collier organised a reunion, when former wireless operator George Wainwright described that descent into darkness. 'Sealand told us that as German aircraft were in the area the lights had been switched off. So it was good luck, and do your best. We thought we'd had it. So we wished each other well, and Toni pulled back the throttle. It was exceedingly bumpy after touchdown, and we couldn't believe we were unhurt.'

As it was, George Wainwright had continued with army co-operation duties, while Antoni Ilnicki had graduated to Lancasters on No. 300 (Masovian) Squadron, finishing the war as a warrant officer with a bar to the prestigious Polish Cross for Valour.

Visiting the Site
Opportunity parking is available just yards from the terminal site, but nothing relevant is to be seen.

7

Hartington

41 MIGNET FLYING FLEA, NEVER REGISTERED (SEE FIGS 73–74)
Hartington

SK 12769 60409 (97 m) Hartington construction site
Owner: Mr Wilshaw Basset
Date: 1935

Mr Ronald Riley, of Hartington, remembered the Flying Flea being constructed in the village. 'Garage owner Wilshaw Basset,' he explained, 'always wanted to build a flying machine, so when the Flying Flea came along he got Walter Birch, from up the Dale, to do all the woodwork. Onlookers would gather about the shed in the evenings, even after the propeller flew off! But eventually the Flea got built, only it wouldn't fly. In the end, they hitched it to a Ford Eight and towed it up to the A515, by the Jug and Glass, to get more breeze. Yet even that didn't do the job. After which they'd exhibit it, driving it around at the local shows. True, at one show a bump threw it about twenty feet into the air, but that was the nearest it got to flying. And then, of course, Flying Fleas were banned as being too dangerous, and that was that. It was stored in the Village Hall and used by the Air Training Corps, then, I rather fancy it was sold off.'

Mr Alan Shipley, of Raikes Farm, Hulme End, who served 22 years in the RAF in the time-honoured, but long-since defunct, trade of blacksmith, was able to supply a photograph of the Hartington Flying Flea.

42 SUPERMARINE SPITFIRE Mᴋ 1 P9563 (ѕᴇᴇ ꜰɪɢѕ 75–76)
Hartington

SK 12449 60750 (231 m) touch down
SK 12490 60480 (231 m) factory yard: former site of the terminal wall
Unit and Station: No. 64 Squadron, RAF Leconfield, No. 11 Group, Fighter Command
Date: 5 September 1940
Crew: pilot, uninjured:
Sergeant D. G. Lloyd

Lost in hazy conditions and short of fuel, Sergeant D. G. Lloyd was unable to correlate ground features and map. In fact, he was 75 miles from his base at Leconfield, Hull, having strayed over Hartington, on the 'wrong' side of the High Peak hills.

Having exhausted all 'lost-procedure' measures, he could have baled out of his very expensive – and infinitely yet more valuable – Spitfire. Instead, he chose to make a precautionary landing on an unprepared field while he still had engine power.

With such a high-performance machine, it was not a decision to be made lightly; nor did he treat it so. As witness, Mr Arthur Kirkham, remembered. 'He circled for quite some time, and came so low over Big Pasture, and then Sich, that we could see him looking down. But finally he edged over and settled on the Big A.'

The 'Big A' was a narrow pasture which, once the wheels cleared the ancient pinch-stones stile at its northern boundary, would have afforded a 300 yard landing run on reasonably flat, if unprepared, ground. A cheese factory, however, baulked any overshoot.

'He came in over the pinchstones,' Mr Kirkham continued, 'bumped, and ran on. Only he couldn't stop and went into the drystone wall. Not the present-day wall, but one that used to be some way back.'

Mr Ronald Riley, another witness, was on the factory roof. 'I was seeing to some cooling coils. Then this Spitfire appeared and began to circle. After about fifteen minutes, though, he landed, but ran out of space and ploughed into the wall in front of me. Though they knew it might have exploded both Joseph Brindley and Arthur Tress jumped up onto the wings to extricate the pilot. He was dazed, so it took them a while to realise that his harness was still secured. But that it didn't catch fire doesn't detract from their bravery. Anyway, the RAF sent a car for the pilot, a guard was mounted overnight, and next day a Queen Mary took the plane away.'

The impact caused substantial damage to the Spitfire, but Sergeant Lloyd emerged unscathed from both crash and inquiry, the accident being attributed jointly to the poor visibility and to his having logged just 120 hours.

Visiting the Site
The terminal-wall site has long been covered by a forecourt, shortening the pasture by some thirty yards. But the ancient pinch-stones are still there, beckoning the walker further afield …

North of Leek

43 MILES MASTER Mk 2 DK912 (SEE FIG 77)
Gipsies' Hollow, Thorncliffe, near Leek, Staffordshire

SK 00730 57220 (240 m)
Unit and Station: No. 17 (Pilots) Advanced Flying Unit, RAF Calveley, near Nantwich,
   Cheshire, No. 21 Group, Flying Training Command,
Date: 13 July 1943
Crew: pilot, unhurt
Sergeant Bernard Francis Lee, Royal Australian Air Force

This pupil pilot became lost, and running short of fuel in misty conditions, set the trainer down. 'It finished up', remembered Mr Martin Glover, of Grove Bank Farm, 'very near the stream and was so badly damaged that it had to be towed away and scrapped. The area was much longer then, but I've put a holly hedge in since.'

Sergeant Lee eventually got his wings and was commissioned as a pilot officer but was killed on fighter operations on 28 September 1944.

Mr Glower also recalled that a Tiger Moth put down in similar circumstances beyond the crossroads at SK 00788 57646 (260 m). In this case there was no damage, so a fuel bowser was sent together with a sergeant instructor, who flew off the aircraft with the understandably shaken pupil. Hedges and buildings have since narrowed the once-generously rectangular site.

Visiting the Site
The Tiger Moth set-down site is beyond the crossroads to the south-west of Thorncliffe. The Master crash site is 450 yards further south, just before the descent to the stream at Gipsies' Hollow.

44 UNIDENTIFIED BIPLANE
Shay Side, Warslow–Onecote Road, Warslow

SK 07790 58140 (260m)
Operator: unknown
Date: *c.* 1935
Occupant: pilot, unidentified

In pointing out where the machine came to rest, Mr William Salt, of Butterton, remembered, 'I cycled over to see this biplane, so it would have been 1935 or so. It merely landed, although whether he had trouble, or got lost in mist, I couldn't say.'

An article in the *Leek Post and Times* of 30 January 1986 suggests the latter, specifying that the French pilot 'calmly took off again before rescuers could reach him ...'

Visiting the Site
There is opportunity parking on the B5053 but, understandably, no evidence to be seen.

45 UNIDENTIFIED BIPLANE (SEE FIG 78)
Budgetts Farm, Butterton

SK 07512 55796 (309 m)
Operator: unknown
Date: *c.* 1927
Occupant: pilot, unidentified, unhurt

Mr William Salt, of Butterton, described this incident. 'It was a light, single-engined biplane. It came down on the pasture just above Budgetts Farm on Pothooks Lane and had to be taken away by road.' The *Leek Post and Times* archives might shed more light.

Visiting the Site
There is opportunity parking on Pothooks Lane.

46 BRISTOL BULLDOG (SEE FIGS 79–80)
Butterton Moor, Onecote–Warslow Road

SK 06271 56750 (355 m)
Unit and Station: No. 3 Flying Training School, RAF Grantham (Spitalgate, from 1944)
Date: 4 January 1936
Crew: pilot, unhurt
Flying Officer Malcolm Stewart

On 4 January 1936 Flying Officer Malcolm Stewart was on route from RAF Grantham, in Lincolnshire, to RAF Seighford, near Stafford, when his engine began to malfunction. He decided to put the machine down, drawing much local attention as he did so.

The field Flying Officer Stewart selected, beside the Onecote–Warslow road, was adequate to the task, but possibly he approached a shade too fast, for he overran into a drystone wall and the machine turned turtle. As the *Leek Post and Times* reported, it was fortunate that the tail fin held the fuselage clear of the ground, so preventing the pilot from being trapped in his cockpit. As it was, a lorry driver drove him into Warslow to a telephone.

Initially, Police Constable Rowley, of Warslow, posted himself as guard, but in the early hours an RAF sergeant and a salvage party arrived to transport the dismantled aircraft back to Grantham, the sergeant having been occupied (*Leek Post*) 'in fending off the host of young men from the surrounding districts who ... stood in awe around the machine.'

'The paper got it wrong,' averred one of that host, Mr William Salt, of Butterton, 'it said it was opposite the Grindon Road whereas it was opposite the Butterton Road.' He added, 'The field was shorter then, the wall he hit having been cleared away. And narrower too, for the lengthways wall was taken out to make one field.'

Visiting the site
The altered field is easily viewed from the B5053, Onecote–Warslow Road.

47 BRISTOL BULLDOG Mk 2A (see figs 81–82)
Onecote Grange Farm, north of Onecote, Leek

SK 04184 55600 (304 m) aircraft impacted
SK 05000 55580 (305 m) pilot parachuted 976/458
Unit and Station: No. 3 Flying Training School, RAF Grantham (Spitalgate, from 1944)
Date: 26 November 1934
Crew: pilot, unhurt, abandoned by parachute
Flight Lieutenant Coombe

Late in the afternoon of 26 November 1934, Flight Lieutenant Coombe became detached from his formation in cloud and realised that he had no idea of his position. However, finding the terrain blotted out by low cloud and mist, he wisely decided that it would be foolhardy to risk a blind descent. Accordingly, as the *Leek Post and Times* reported, 'He climbed to 4,000 feet and made a daring jump in a parachute.'

Flight Lieutenant Coombe came safely to earth on the northern boundary of Onecote, some three miles east of Leek, touching down on Fold Farm's Thistle Pasture. His abandoned machine, meanwhile, plunged into a field belonging to Onecote Grange Farm, to the north-west of the village.

Farmer Mr Critchlow reported that shortly after he had heard the engine cut off, the machine had nose-dived from the clouds at a great speed, burying itself in the ground. Running to give aid, he had found it empty.

Mr Joe Arnitt, of Blowoerem [Blow over them] Farm, smiled. 'I was talking to the council roadmender when we heard this bang. He looked up, saw the parachute, and said, "Look there! Here the bugger comes in a piece of the plane!"'

In like vein, Mr Robert Poyser, of Fold Farm, recalled that farmworker Mr Harold Brassington, having asked the pilot where the plane was, maintained that he had been told, 'The bugger's off over there somewhere.'

Next day, the local newspaper congratulated itself that, 'Once again the *Leek Post and Times* reporters were first on the scene … their photographs showing that the aircraft was completely embedded in the ground … only the tail and under-carriage could be seen.' It also explained to its readers that the machine had 'smashed without the engine running, which fact, of course, explained why the machine did not burst into flames.'

In fact, Flight Lieutenant Coombe, finding himself lost above cloud, would have used his time in searching for a gap through which he might either pinpoint himself or make a precautionary landing. Indeed, only as the fuel-starved engine died would he have taken to his parachute.

And having telephoned his base from Leek police station? As the attentive reporters recorded, Flight Lieutenant Coombe 'waited until the express 'bus left for Derby, on which he then travelled …'

Visiting the Site
Roadside opportunity parking can be found nearby but the impact site, on private farmland, was excavated in the 1990s, leaving no surface evidence.

48 DESOUTTER Mk 1 G-AAPZ (see fig 83)
Stockmeadows Farm, Meerbrook

SJ 97963 61900 (263 m)
Owner: National Flying Services, Hanworth
Date: 12 July 1934
Occupant: pilot, Flight Lieutenant J. B. Wilson

The set-down was witnessed by Mr Tom Hine, who described it to his son, Mr David Hine, of Thorneyleigh Hall Farm. 'Dad would say, "This aeroplane suddenly appeared out of the mist," He'd then explain that the pilot kept off the ground too long and had to hop over the stone wall, crashing beside the quarry. Nobody was hurt, but the aeroplane had to be dismantled and taken off by road.'

The Dessoutter had been engaged in the preliminary stages of the prestigious King's Cup air race when it developed engine trouble, obliging Flight Lieutenant Wilson to set it down, the damage then suffered forcing its retirement.

G-AAPZ first flew on 18 August 1931. In 1935 it joined what was to become the Shuttleworth Trust, and in early 2012, aged eighty-one, and some years after a prolonged rebuild, it was still flying at Old Warden!

Visiting the Site
The site is handily accessed from Meerbrook, with public footpaths running through Lower Wetwood Farm. Since the Desoutter crashed, however, the quarry has been considerably extended, swallowing the site shown on the contemporary photograph

49 MILES MAGISTER L8139 (see figs 84–85)
Stockmeadows Farm, Meerbrook

SJ 98371 61955 (227 m) struck tree
Unit and Station: No. 5 Elementary Flying Training School, RAF Ternhill, Market Drayton
Date: 20 April 1941
Crew: pilot, survived precautionary landing
Leading Aircraftman J. W. Aston, RAF Volunteer Reserve

Pupil pilot Leading Aircraftman Aston became lost in misty conditions during a solo mapreading cross-country exercise, and seeing the rugged tops of the Roaches ahead, decided to land before fuel too became a problem. Overflying a farmhouse – a farm representing communications and succour – he aimed for a field that happened to be on the lower slopes of Gun Hill. Possibly the gradient upset his judgement, for he struck a tree, damaging the machine but suffering only superficial injuries himself.

No disciplinary action was taken, for getting lost was a hazard attendant upon elementary flying training, and the pupil had showed a level head in putting down in good time.

Visiting the Site
The field, chosen also by the 1934 Desoutter (see above, and for visiting details), is the central one of a trio forming a distinctive pattern visible for miles, some 350 yards west of Stockmeadows Farm, but presently belonging to Lower Wetwood Farm.

50 HAWKER HART K3864 (SEE FIG 86)
Barleigh Ford Bridge, north of Rushton Spencer

SJ 94310 63784 (142 m)
Unit and Station: No. 28 Elementary and Reserve Flying Training School, No. 50 Group, Meir
    Airfield, Stoke on Trent
Operator: Reid & Sigrist Ltd, for the RAF Volunteer Reserve
Date: 27 May 1939
Occupant: pilot, killed
Sergeant Clare Norman Parish, RAF Volunteer Reserve

Mrs Mabel Goodfellow, of Wormhill Farm, Rushton Spencer, was able to describe what happened on 27 May 1939 when Sergeant Clare Parish decided to carry out an unauthorised display of low-level aerobatics.

'He had been showing off to friends in Barleighford Farm,' she recalled, 'looping-the-loop, and diving and climbing. But he eventually got too low, and crashed into the trees. My husband always said he'd been fooling about.'

The 1939 incumbent of the adjacent property, Mr Eric Eardley, had also been a witness.

'The pilot,' he said, 'had friends just across the River Dane, and he'd regularly come over on Sundays, and stunt. So us kids'd sit on the wall and watch the show. He was very daring, but on this occasion he got too low, and the downdraft sucked him into the trees. He hit where the footpath now crosses the bad bend just over the bridge.'

The inquiry established that Sergeant Parish had dived out of one manoeuvre straight into a turn. From which it can be deduced that, as the trees loomed, he hurriedly tried to gain height, only to pull into the performance-killing judder of a high-speed stall, at once losing turning capability, lift, and as the machine struck, life itself.

Visiting the Site
The site is accessed by heading north from Rushton Spencer to Barleigh Ford Bridge. It is a fine walking area, but there is nothing to be seen at the crash site, on the public footpath, just above the bridge.

51 SUPERMARINE SPITFIRE
Little Bradshaw Farm, Bradshaw, near Rudyard

SJ 94341 56280 (157 m)
Unit and Station: An unidentified Spitfire Operational Training Unit
Date: 1942–3
Crew: pilot, unidentified, unhurt

While on a training sortie, a pilot from a Spitfire Operational Training Unit became lost and, as the light faded, chose to make a precautionary landing in a field directly below Little Bradshaw Farm. However, he misjudged the gradient in the gloom, touched down too far into the field, went through a hedge, and rolled onwards into a deep pit.

At the time, Mr Brian Shufflebotham lived with his parents at Bradshaw Park. 'We'd heard this thunderous roar,' he remembered, 'as an aircraft went very low overhead. Then, perhaps two hours later, there was this knock at the door. Dad, an ARP warden, took down the butt-loading revolver he'd brought back from the First World War and opened the door. Only to find an RAF pilot, fully kitted in leather jacket and helmet.'

Mr Shufflebotham smiled. 'It turned out that nobody had heard him actually crash. So when he arrived at Little Bradshaw Farm they thought he was a fifth columnist, and sent him up to dad, their landlord. That is, they left him, shocked though he must have been, to find his own way uphill through the pitch-dark woods to totally blacked-out Bradshaw Park!'

He paused. 'We'd got a telephone, though, so after a while he was taken back to his unit. The police and RAF cordoned off the area and eventually carted away the wreckage in Queen Mary trailers ...'

Visiting the Site
The site is just off Dunwood Lane, between Bradshaw and Lyme House. In 2012, the hollow had long been used as a tip, with no hope of any aircraft debris being discovered.

9

South of Leek

52 AVRO ANSON K6283 (see fig 87)
Bradnop, near Leek

SK 02345 55501 (337 m)
Unit and Station: No. 2 School of Air Navigation, No. 21 Group, Flying Training Command
Date: 17 February 1941
Crew: three, pilot killed, two crew members survived, injured
Sergeant Arthur Maelor Owen, RAF Volunteer Reserve, pilot, killed
Pilot Officer W. P. Ferrie, RAFVR, navigator, injured
Flight Sergeant A. H. Judkins, RAFVR, wireless operator, injured

Sergeant Arthur Owen and his crew were engaged in a navigational exercise employing dead (deduced) reckoning techniques when they became seriously 'uncertain of their position' – a navigators' euphemism for being lost. Just as they were calling for radio-navigational assistance, however, the cloud opened to reveal ground features. Sergeant Owen immediately descended, only to discover that he had fallen into the 'sucker's-gap' trap, the cloud immediately closing up around him. It became obvious too that he had descended into a valley, with a moorland shoulder looming up unavoidably just moments later. Sergeant Owen was killed, the other two crew members injured, and the Anson destroyed.

The court of inquiry found that Sergeant Owen had committed an error of judgement in descending 'in order to carry out a forced-landing', with the failure to obtain radio-navigational aid being a contributory factor. Strange reasoning, for the only time he might have considered setting down was in the moments before impact when he realised his predicament.

Notwithstanding which, a human touch – almost unprecedented in RAF crash reports – was supplied when Sergeant Owen's commanding officer observed that it had been 'bad luck in that the clear patch was in a valley', conceding too that 'conditions had been difficult'.

Mr Ivan Rogers was able to point out where the Anson crashed. 'It was largely very thin plywood,' he remembered. 'But the tail was sticking up out of the ditch. And it hadn't burnt.'

Visiting the Site
The crash site is on private land belonging to Brook Farm, high on the moor above and to the east of Bradnop village, and on what can be unbelievably boggy moorland. Although debris scraps were found after some ditching work, there is normally nothing to be seen.

53 DE HAVILLAND PUSS MOTH G-AAZW (SEE FIG 88)
Roughstone Hole, Bradnop, Leek

SK 01838 53116 (261 m)
Operator: private owner
Date: 23 November 1934
Crew: pilot, killed
Mr Geoffrey Heap Turner

Mr Geoffrey Turner, a member of a Rochdale cotton manufacturing family, was returning from a jaunt to Geneva in his de Havilland Puss Moth. He had cleared customs in Southampton and, during a stop at London's Heston aerodrome, had arranged to have his chauffeur meet him at Barton, Manchester. However, at Roughstone Hole, just outside Leek, in Staffordshire, he crashed in fog, the Moth bursting into flames. Mr Turner, trapped in the wreckage, did not survive.

Mr Archibald Cantrell, of Roughstone Hole Farm, told the coroner's court that he had been standing by his house, situated half-way up the slope above Combes Brook, when he had become aware of an aeroplane which, by the sound of its engine, seemed to be circling further along the mist-filled Combes Valley, towards Cheddleton. He described how the machine had suddenly loomed through the mist only fifty yards off, still with its engine going, but heading for the hillside. Awestruck, he could do nothing but watch as its wing struck a drystone wall and the whole machine burst into flames.

The heat was far too intense for him to even attempt to approach, so after a while he turned away and despondently set about raising the alarm.

First on the scene were reporters from the *Leek Post and Times* who, finding a smouldering attaché case, were able to identify the pilot. All that was left of the machine, they recorded, were, 'metal stays, the engine, [and the] petrol tank.'

Flight Lieutenant Davey, of the Accidents Branch of the Air Ministry, told the coroner's court that there had been no indication of any mechanical malfunction. Moreover, his responses to questions cast singular light upon the terrain-clearance practices of the day: practices that would remain the norm until well after the Second World War. In this context, it should be noted that the Roughstone Hole crash site is at an elevation of some 900 feet above sea level.

'Was the machine fitted with altitude recorders?' the coroner asked.

'The recorder,' Flight Lieutenant Davey replied, 'would show his height to be 900 feet and he would think he was safe. That's what makes me think he was lost.'

'What should have been his normal altitude?' pressed the coroner.

'A reasonable height is five hundred feet above the highest land point, so fifteen hundred feet would have been quite safe.'

In contrast, since the late forties the minimum safety height for the route would have been 3,600 feet!

As it was, Mr Turner's altimeter, set to read above near-sea-level Heston, would have given a relatively accurate reading on arriving over near-sea-level Barton. In the Leek area, however, when he circled around in low cloud trying to re-locate himself, 900 feet on his altimeter actually meant that he had been skimming the ground! Indeed, beyond the actual impact point the ground above Roughstone Hole rises yet another 160 feet!

As the coroner observed to the jury, 'This was purely a case of a man losing his way in the fog and dashing into a wall on the side of Morridge [the general hill mass] … he thought he was well up.'

Mrs Doris Sales had lived at nearby Gorstead Mill Farm since 1939, when the tragedy was still fresh. She tendered, 'They brought the pilot on a door to Roughstone Hole – or Hall, as it is now.'

Visiting the Site

Although a footpath passes close, the site is in a family's back garden, and no evidence of the incident remains.

54 MILES MASTER Mᴋ 3 W8840 (sᴇᴇ ꜰɪɢs 89–90)
Bottom House, Ashbourne–Leek Road

SK 04384 52216 (293 m)
Unit and Station: No. 7 Ferry Pilots Pool, Sherburn-in-Elmet, Air Transport Auxiliary,
    Maintenance Command.
Date: 15 January 1943
Crew: pilot, killed
First Officer Thomas Henry Williams, Air Transport Auxiliary

Just thirty minutes into an 80-mile ferry flight from RAF Sherburn-in-Elmet, south-west of York, to RAF Ternhill, near Market Drayton, Shropshire, Air Transport Auxiliary (ATA) pilot First Officer Thomas Williams was killed when he ran into bad weather, lost control, and dived into the ground at Bottom House, Staffordshire.

ATA Ferry Rules dictated that a pilot should turn back if bad weather could not be avoided. The inquiry, therefore, had to find that, 'the pilot committed an error of judgement in proceeding too far into unforeseen bad weather conditions'.

Asked about the crash, Farmer Mr Fred Gee instantly responded, 'It happened on 15 January 1943!' As he explained, though, 'It was the day my wife, Kathleen, was born – her parents, the Mycocks, farming this place at that time.' He went on, 'The aircraft made a deep crater in what was little more than a marsh. Until thirty years back when I ditched and drained it, backfilling it with rubbish.'

Visiting the Site

The site is beside a public footpath that leads off the A523 just eastwards of Bottom House, but nothing is to be seen.

*Airspeed Oxford DF408,
Dawson Farm
See page 66*

Top: **60.** The site of the
impact and onward slide of
Oxford DF408, recalled by
Mrs Evelyn Naden.

*Douglas C-47 Skytrain, Dawson Farm
See page 67*

61. The impact site.

62. (Inset) Francis Nade, shown with the oak leaves of the Kings Commendation, braved the flames.

Flying Flea G-ADVU, Congleton
See page 69

63. The crash site of the Flying Flea at Congleton.

64. (Insct) An airborne Flying Flea.

Vickers Wellington Mk 3 Z1744, Hen Cloud
See page 71

Top: **65.** The impact point of Wellington Z1744. The terminal point is beyond the lowest section of the trees.

Supermarine Spitfire P7593, Windygates
See page 72

Top: **66.** The impact site of Spitfire P7593.

Below **67.** The excavated engine of P7593 at Thorpe Camp Aviation Museum.

Airspeed Oxford V3636, Fawside Edge
See page 73

Bottom **68.** The impact point.

English Electric Canberra B Mk 6 WT207, Monyash
See page 74

69. The site of the RAF camp set up at Monyash.

Westland Lysander V9729, Sparklow
See page 76

Bottom **70.** The Royal Oak from the terminal wall.

71. (Inset) Westland Lysander.

72. Mr and Mrs Bill and Irene Cole indicate the terminal site of Lysander V9729.

Flying Flea, Hartington
See page 77

73. Mr Ronald Riley of Hartington shows where the Flea was constructed.

74. (Inset) Testing a Flying Flea.

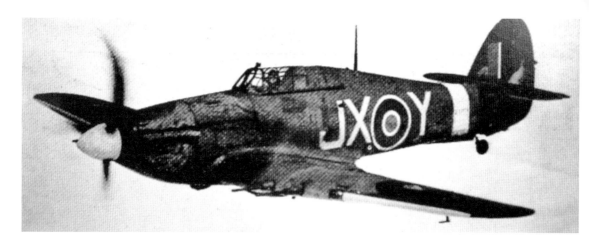

Suprmarine Spitfire Mk 1 P9563, Hartington
See page 78

75. Supermarine Spitfire.

76. The area of the old stone wall and impact site of Spitfire P9563, looking back along the line of approach.

Miles Master Mk 2 DK912, Gipsies' Hollow
See page 79

77. The set-down area of Master DK912, falling away towards Gipsies' Hollow.

Unidentified biplane, Budgetts Farm
See page 80

78. The set-down field of the biplane in 1927, looking back along the line of flight, towards Butterton.

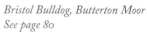

Bristol Bulldog, Butterton Moor
See page 80

Top: **79.** Bristol Bulldog.

Middle: **80.** Mr William Salt indicates the site where the Bulldog crashed in January 1936.

Bristol Bulldog Mk 2A, Onecote Grange Farm
See page 81

Bottom: **81.** The impact site of another Bulldog from 1934, looking towards Onecote Grange Farm

82. (inset) Thistle Pasture, Fold Farm, into which the pilot parachuted.

Desoutter Mk 1 G-AAPZ, Stockmeadows Farm
See page 82

83. Local historian Mrs Sheila Hine at the crash site of Desoutter G-AAPZ, the distinctive east–west fields falling to the right being those chosen by the Desoutter pilot and, years later, by a Magister pilot.

Miles Magister L8139, Stockmeadows Farm
See page 82

84. Miles Magister.

85. The touchdown area with the tree line that Magister L8139 struck. Beyond is the field that the Desoutter overran, hopping the far wall, then crashing.

Hawker Hart K3864, Barleigh Ford Bridge
See page 83

Top: **86.** The crash site of Hawker Hart K3864, from Barleigh Ford Bridge.

Avro Anson K6283, Bradnop
See page 84

Middle: **87.** Avro Anson.

De Havilland Puss Moth G-AAZW, Roughstone Hole
See page 85

Bottom: **88.** The drystone wall where Puss Moth G-AAZW crashed.

10

Grindon

55 DOUGLAS C-53D SKYTROOPER 42-68728 (SEE FIG 91–92)
Ossoms Hill, Grindon

SK 09275 55386 (327 m) initial touchdown area
SK 09200 55576 (316 m) terminal area
Unit and Station: United States Ninth Army Air Force, 78th Troop Carrier Squadron, 435rd
    Troop Carrier Group, 9th Tactical Control Center, AAF490 (RAF Langar), Nottinghamshire
Date: 13 January 1944
Occupants: nine, all United States Army Air Force, superficial injuries
First Lieutenant Edward M. St John, pilot
Second Lieutenant Calvin H. White, co-pilot
Second Lieutenant Robert L. Delancey, navigator
Staff Sergeant John F. Griffith, Flight Engineer
Corporal Raymond F. Brandt, radio operator
First Officer Russell R. Ford, passenger
Staff Sergeant Sidney D. Wax, passenger
Sergeant Junior Jeremiah, passenger
Sergeant J. Vacarro, passenger

When First Lieutenant Edward St John and his crew were tasked to carry out a flight to the American facility at Burtonwood, he maintained 600 feet above the hills. On encountering moderate turbulence he prudently reduced his speed, but just as he approached Ossoms Hill, his right wing-tip crumpled. Finding the aircraft's handling properties markedly affected, he carried out a wheels-up emergency landing, but although he chose the only flat land available he struck three field-dividing drystone walls before stopping.

Subsequent specialist investigation of the wing-tip showed that its internal structure had been damaged by contact with another C-53's wing-tip during some taxying or towing operation. Accordingly the accident was attributed to structural failure, and one would hope First Lieutenant St John received plaudits for a job well done.

The shaken occupants arrived at Ossoms Hill Farm, to be bedded down on the floor while awaiting transport and medical checks. Two crew members, though, walked down to Wetton Mill to find a phone and on drawing blank, laboured on uphill to Wetton.

Mrs Frances Salt (née Gibbs) remembered their arrival. 'We used to congregate around the telephone kiosk – it had a light. But this night these two big men just appeared in front of us. We gawped. We'd no notion of a plane crash. They were dressed in brown bomber jackets and leather helmets, with ear muffs. And got very frustrated trying to get through. "We hit one stone fence," we heard them telling someone, "Then another fence, and landed on a third." *Fences*, they called them!'

Mrs Salt described what she found next day. 'There was this plane, hardly damaged, on level ground, but just before it sloped to the cliff. We kids got inside. And my brother, Ray, took a bit of perspex, and made rings of it which he sold for tuppence or thruppence. In fact, I had mine for years …'

It was fondly remembered, too, that the American salvage crew gave away the aviation fuel with the neighbourly admonition that it should be mixed with paraffin before being used in vehicles.

Farmer Arthur Coates, a veteran of Dunkirk and Normandy, pointed out the wall sections demolished by the aircraft. 'I rebuilt them on coming home', he observed with justifiable pride, 'and they've been standing now for fifty-odd years.'

Visiting the Site
Great views, but the incident has left no trace.

56 VICKERS WELLINGTON Mk 3 Z1566 (see figs 93–94)
Sheldon Farm, Grindon, Staffordshire

SK 06779 55070 (365 m)
Unit and Station: No. 75 Squadron, Royal New Zealand Air Force, RAF Feltwell, near Ely, No.
   3 Group, Bomber Command
Date: 23 May 1942
Crew: six, five killed, one survived, injured
Pilot Officer Andrew Donald Mackay, RNZAF, pilot, killed
Sergeant Wilfred Hubert Smeaton, RNZAF, observer [navigator], killed
Sergeant J. W. Bode, RAF, observer [navigator], killed
Sergeant J. W. Beaven, RNZAF, wireless operator/air gunner, killed
Sergeant C. Hayton, RNZAF, air gunner, killed
Sergeant Sydney John Chappell, RNZAF, rear gunner, injured

Towards the end of a training sortie, Pilot Officer Andrew McKay and his Royal New Zealand Air Force crew became uncertain of their position. The navigators advised of nearby ground rising to 1,500 feet above sea level, but after some discussion Pilot Officer McKay decided to descend blind to fix their position. And at 0330 hours the aircraft crashed beside Sheldon Farm, near Grindon, killing five crew members. The surviving rear gunner, Sergeant Sydney Chappell, though injured, extracted himself from a muck pit and crawled to the farmhouse to arouse the occupants.

As Mr Graham Simpson, of Oldfield Farm, remembered, 'At first, Frank Chadwick, the farmer, thought he was a German, and took the shotgun to him.' He paused reflectively. 'You really have to pity that airman,' he said then, 'Injured, all his mates dead. And before the electric came, as dark as a bag up here.'

'The aeroplane,' Mr William Salt, of Butterton, recalled, 'was facing south-east with the left wing up, the right one dug into the ground, and the tail hinged back to the right.'

Having Sergeant Chappell's testimony, the court of inquiry had little to do, finding that Pilot Officer McKay had descended blind despite being warned of the proximity of high ground.

There is, however, an unusual dimension to this narrative. In 1999, when Mrs Cynthia Bullock came to Sheldon Farm, she knew all about the Halifax bomber that crashed nearby in 1947 (see page 24) but she had no notion of another crash.

'On this particular night, however,' she said, not without reluctance, 'disturbed by the thunder and lightning, I looked out. And there was this airman standing in the yard.' She pursed her lips.

'I couldn't call to my husband to look, for there was nothing to be seen … Not seen as such …'

David, her former-policeman husband, supplemented this evidence of his wife's sensitivity, 'And from the start Cynthia was always uncomfortable about the old stone barn.'

Mrs Bullock being a level-headed schoolteacher, however, the experience began to fade, but not her uneasiness over the barn. Until some five years later when the aforementioned Graham Simpson, doing a job at the farm, happened to mention the Wellington crash …

And her unaccounted-for discomfort with the barn? He was able to advise that, as in the nearby 1947 crash, the bodies of the crew had been laid out in the nearest shelter. In this case, the old stone barn …

Visiting the Site

Although debris still emerges, the crash site was thoroughly dug over by enthusiasts in the 1980s so nothing is to be seen.

11

Cheddleton

57 CONSOLIDATED VULTEE B-24H LIBERATOR 42-52625 (FIG 95)
Brown Edge, Leek

SJ 91277 54193 (240 m) farmyard tree, second impact point
SJ 91491 54034 (232 m) terminal crash site
Unit and Station: United States Eighth Army Air Force, 492nd Bomber Group, 406th Bomber Squadron, AAF113 (RAF Cheddington), south-west of Luton
Date: 15 August 1944
Crew: five, and one passenger, all survived, some injuries
Second Lieutenant Tommie F. Leftwich, pilot
Second Lieutenant John A. Majdick, co-pilot
Second Lieutenant Woodrow Klauber, navigator, fractured leg
Sergeant Ralph H. Sandmeyer, radio operator, burned hands
Sergeant David P. Christie, flight engineer; bruised chest
Corporal Grace M. Sharkey, Women's Army Corps, passenger, slight cuts

Second Lieutenant Tommie Leftwich had taken a reduced crew to ferry a newly modified Liberator from RAF Warton – then American Base Air Depot No. 2 – near Blackpool, to their base at RAF Cheddington, near Luton. Corporal Grace Sharkey, a Women's Air Corps nurse, went along for the ride.

Fifty minutes after take-off, the aircraft was seen to circle a cricket ground at Knypersley, near Leek, then to hit a tree on the ridge beyond. Passing out of sight of the cricket crowd, it then crashed and caught fire at Morris House Farm, the occupants evacuating safely, albeit with some minor injuries.

In fact, the flight had been traumatic from the outset. On leaving Warton, the undercarriage had been reluctant to retract. But having sorted that out, as Second Lieutenant Leftwich's report testifies, 'The response to control inputs was jerky, and excessive trim was needed to keep the machine on course.'

On occasion it seemed reluctant to answer corrections at all, and over Knypersley – as it happened – it suddenly performed a self-initiated circle to the left despite any contrary input he applied. At this he decided to return to Warton, except that when he banked left to do so the aircraft entered a dive.

The two pilots managed to get the nose up, but the aircraft still struck a tree. This damaged the tailplane and also the right-inner engine, which cut and burst into flames. Second Lieutenant Leftwich managed to ease the machine over a ridge but then found that neither his rudder nor his elevator would answer.

'The plane was going sideways,' runs his report to the police, written the next morning, 'And I could get no control over it. We hit the ground on our right wing, in doing so the plane turned around and skidded backwards.' A day later, however, verbatim extracts from his official report attest: 'Knowing that I had two people in the nose, and no one in the tail I decided to turn the plane around when hitting. Leaving number four throttle off [the right-outer engine], and leaving numbers one and two on … swung the plane around just before we hit the ground.' Clearly the second version casts him in a more controlling role!

The prime concern of the investigators, however, was to determine whether the aircraft had really acted so temperamentally, or whether the accident had been caused by irresponsible flying. Witnesses at the cricket ground, though, testified that the aircraft had clearly been experiencing difficulties. On that head, then, the investigators found that inquiries 'strongly eliminate [the] possibility of intentional low flying or "buzzing"'.

As it transpired, wider investigations showed that other newly-modified B24s had suffered similar stability problems, particularly in the ferry role when they were loaded slightly aft of centre. It was concluded, therefore, that the accident was 'directly attributable to [the] instability of [the] flight control surfaces due to modification', the cause being 'Aircraft Structure, 100%, Pilot Error, none'.

Mr Harry Painter of Morris House Farm recalled the crash itself. 'The plane struck a tree just beyond the farmhouse and part of its wing fell off. After that the rest spun around and slid backwards down to the far end of the field, shedding other bits as it went. When it came to a stop there was only one engine still attached, and that was on fire, but all the crew got out safely.'

What intrigued Mr Painter was to see a folded daily newspaper inside the turret, also an opened packet of biscuits. He was also intrigued by the guns, 'Still wrapped in greaseproof paper.' But he remembered too how burning fuel had leaked into the field drains, so that his family were hard put to save a nearby crop.

Mr Bratt, the local butcher, always claimed to be the first on the scene, his son-in-law remembered, and would tell how, having rushed to try to rescue the occupants, he had been beaten back by the heat only to realise that the crew were sitting on the nearby drystone wall, placidly watching him.

'Though Lord knows how he could have been first on the scene,' scoffed a contemporary, 'him with his wooden leg.'

The report of WAC nurse Corporal Grace Sharkey, though, illumined the anguish suffered by any aircraft occupant whose station renders them powerless to affect the outcome. 'I just kept looking straight ahead watching the ground coming up to meet me …'

Visiting the Site

A footpath from Endon Bank passes the site. Alternatively, the Brown Edge Road runs north from the B5051, after which there is lay-by parking on Broad Lane at SJ 91366 53889. A footpath then leads some 400 yards to the field gate and the terminal site. There may be no surface debris, but the sheltering wall remains.

58 MILES MAGISTER Mᴋ 1 L8258
Area of Brund Lane, Cheddleton, Staffordshire

Date: 4 September 1940
Crew: Pilot, unknown, unhurt

Magister L8258 suffered an engine failure and hit overhead cables in its descent, the pilot emerging unhurt. Very likely this is the Magister recorded by Marshall S. Boylan (page 59 of *A Moorland Dedication*) that leaked fuel over crops in Brund Lane. Canvassing the area's longest-term residents stirred no memories, however.

59 DE HAVILLAND MOSQUITO Mᴋ 20 KB206 (ѕᴇᴇ ꜰɪɢѕ 96–97)
Cheddleton Heath, Leek

SJ 98592 53218 (192 m)
Unit and Station: Navigation Training Unit, Pathfinder Force, RAF Warboys, north-east of
    Huntingdon, No. 8 Group, Bomber Command
Date: 2 March 1945
Crew: two, both killed
Flight Lieutenant Arthur Ian Albertson, RAF, pilot
Flight Sergeant Robert James Eaton, Royal Australian Air Force, navigator

Debris spread
Main section (fuselage) fell SJ 98592 53218 (192 m)
Tail SJ 98889 53720 (144 m)
Debris spray in Ashenhurst Park SJ 00180 54198 (195 m)
Cockpit canopy, 'Four-lanes-end' SJ 98799 53302 (167 m)
Debris on the (former) heath SJ 98593 53385 (194 m)
Pilot's parachute, Fynneylane pasture SJ 99598 53625 (208 m)
Pilot SJ 99067 53704 (155 m)
Navigator SJ 98534 53320 (193 m)

Flight Lieutenant Arthur Albertson had logged over 3,000 hours when, two hours into a night-navigation exercise, he and his navigator, Flight Sergeant Robert Eaton, RAAF, were killed after Mosquito KB206 broke up at 27,000 feet. The puzzled investigators were left with a one-and-a-half mile trail of debris around the Cheddleton Heath area, just outside Leek.

'There was this odd noise,' Mr and Mrs Isaac and Doris Hudson of Fynneylane Farm remembered, 'and we realised that a plane had come down near the Cheddleton Heath Road. When we brought Tilley lamps there, though, the RAF had already arrived, so we assumed they'd been pre-warned that the aircraft was in trouble.'

Mr Basil Cooper, then living at nearby Spicers Stone, ran to the site with his brother. 'We came across some debris in the woods, but a lot more near our Uncle Albert Ferniough's bungalow by the road. What we didn't realise is that at Bull Banks we'd passed by one of the bodies.'

It was apparent that both crew members had been thrown through the perspex hood, neither being able to use his parachute. Flight Lieutenant Albertson's canopy, ripped from its pack by some projection, had fouled the tailplane. And even when it had torn free, the badly damaged harness had come apart. The canopy was found draped across the front pasture of Fynneylane Farm but Flight Lieutenant Albertson's body, just downslope of the pasture, was not discovered until the next day. Navigator Flight Sergeant Eaton, for his part, had fallen on the (then) moorland slope, quite close to the main fuselage.

'We found it strange that neither airman was wearing uniform,' Mrs Hudson observed, 'and both had low shoes on, not flying boots.'

'But wreckage fell everywhere,' said Mr Hudson. 'The tail was down by a barn off Basford Lane, just near the pilot.' 'The cockpit cover,' his wife added, 'was stuck up in a tree just below what we call Four-Lane Ends.'

'The RAF recovery crews,' Mr Hudson resumed, 'sent the wreckage to Ashbourne along the track – it's now only a bridleway – between Fynneylane and Ashenhurst Hall Farms.'

The court of inquiry concluded that an oxygen leak had rendered the pilot semi-conscious, probably causing him to collapse against the stick, so sending the aircraft into a series of gyrations that had catastrophically overstressed it.

Mr Basil Cooper was one of many children who fabricated rings and pendants from the perspex. 'We'd heat up the poker in the open fire, then pierce it through – I can smell it to this day! Then we'd grind it on a stone.'

Visiting the Sites
Roads and tracks serve all the locations and considerably chosen opportunity parking is available. However, no visible traces remain, indeed, the fuselage impact site has long been used as a tip.

60 REPUBLIC P-47D THUNDERBOLT 42-74728 (SEE FIGS 98–100)
Greenway Hall, Bagnall, Stoke

SJ 91936 50646 (216 m) abandoned aircraft crashed
SJ 94605 57410 (183 m) pilot parachuted
Unit and Station: 551st Fighter Training Squadron, 495th Fighter Training Group, United States
　　Eighth Army Air Force, AAF342 (RAF Atcham), 5 miles east of Shrewsbury
Date: 29 August 1944
Crew: pilot, baled out, but died of injuries
Second Lieutenant Paul R. Fulton, United States Army Air Force

When two single-seater P-47 pilots were briefed to fly an instrument and aerobatic sortie, they organised themselves so that while the first concentrated 'eyes-down' on instruments, the second kept watch for other aircraft. At intervals they would change roles, marking the changeover with various aerobatic manoeuvres – 'acrobatics', as Second Lieutenant Walker, the number two, has it. It was clearly a productive sortie during which the two of them were also having a very good time.

After forty-five minutes, however, following an aerobatic interlude, Second Lieutenant Walker lost his leader. Receiving no response to his calls, he carried out a search until his fuel ran low, when he returned to base.

The Shufflebotham family, of Bradshaw Park, to the south of Rudyard, had become aware of the activity above them. 'Suddenly,' Mr Brian Shufflebotham recalled, 'we heard one begin a dive which just seemed to go on and on. Until there was a distant thump – and then silence. Then, long minutes later, mother exclaimed, "There's the pilot!" and pointed to a parachute drifting our way from the south-west, from Gratton. It was very high still, indeed mother had time to fetch the binoculars. "He's not moving," she said worriedly, "He's just hanging limply."

'The parachute drifted past us,' Mr Shufflebotham continued, 'so one of my brothers and I ran straight through the yard of Steel House Farm and up the track to the brow of the hill beyond. There were several people there but the pilot was just lying on his back, groaning, and pleading, "Doctor – please …" Only he died before the doctor arrived.'

The American investigators quickly concluded that Second Lieutenant Fulton – a day-fighter pilot with just four hundred hours – had lost control while in cloud. Further, having examined his parachute, they deduced that he had left his attempt at recovery too long, only baling out when the dive had reached an abnormally high speed. Even then, instead of waiting for the speed to stabilise somewhat, he had immediately pulled the ripcord, the canopy deploying with such force as to snap his spine. The conclusion had to be 'one hundred per cent pilot error', the major cause poor technique, the minor poor judgement.

The aircraft itself had dived into shrubland three miles away at Greenway Hall, near Stockton Brook, beside what has long been the tenth fairway of the Greenway Hall Golf Club. Mr George Phillips, then the janitor at nearby Bagnall Hospital, was the first to reach it, dreading what he would find, only to discover an empty cockpit.

Visiting the Site

There is lay-by parking on the Baddeley Edge Road at SJ 92120 50567, but on a very fast and dangerously unsighted bend! At the site itself scraps do emerge, although an excavation was carried out in the 1980s.

12
Cellarhead

61 ENGLISH ELECTRIC CANBERRA B Mk 2 WH669 (SEE FIG 101)
Whitehurst Farm, Dilhorne, near Cellarhead, Staffordshire

SJ 97280 45647 (219 m)
Unit and Station: No. 10 Squadron, RAF Scampton, Lincolnshire, No. 1 Group, Bomber
   Command
Date: 27 March 1953
Crew: Three, all killed
Flying Officer Patrick Edmund Reeve, pilot
Pilot Officer John Golden Woods, navigator/plotter
Pilot Officer Vivian Owen, navigator/observer

Flying Officer Patrick Reeve and his crew had overshot from an instrument approach at Scampton and climbed to the west. Flying Officer Reeve's intention seems to have been to commence another homing, descent, and approach from 30,000 feet. However, just minutes later, and sixty-three miles distant, the Canberra dived vertically into the ground near Cheadle, leaving no survivors.

('Only ten minutes? From Lincolnshire,' exclaimed the coroner. 'Good heavens!')

The investigators established that WH669 had been inverted when it struck, that it had maintained its integrity until impact, then burst into flames. There had been no emergency call, no evidence of mechanical or structural failure, or of either carbon monoxide poisoning or anoxia [lack of oxygen – later re-termed hypoxia]. It was clear, though, that measures had been taken to slow the machine, for the airbrakes had been extended and the bomb-bay doors opened. Just the same, although the pilot's canopy had been jettisoned, none of the crew had attempted to eject.

In fact, in an endeavour to find some definite cause for the accident, public appeals were made for any souvenirs to be returned for examination.

In the event, the inquiry had to submit that Flying Officer Reeve had lost control at high altitude while flying on instruments, conceivably after he had stopped an engine to practise engine failure, only to mishandle the asymmetric condition, fall into cloud, then enter a high-speed spiral dive.

When he crashed Flying Officer Reeve had 400 flying hours, just 68 on type, and a meagre four on instruments. Even more significantly, he claimed only three hours in the last six months spent flying solely with reference to instruments, very few of which would have been spent in exercising, 'Recovery from Unusual Attitudes'.

When the Canberra crashed, Mrs Marjorie Mears, née Wheat, was a child living at Whitehurst Farm. 'Dad,' she recalled, 'had been gathering up eggs, and hearing the plane coming down thought it was going to land on him. Once it crashed, though, he rushed across, but there was nothing he could do, other than get back and contact the police.'

Visiting the Site

Permission will, of course, be sought at the farm. A few scraps of debris may be found in the hedgerow by the impact site.

13
Cheadle

62 MILES MAGISTER Mᴋ 1 L5950
Blakelow Farm, Draycott in the Moors, Staffordshire

SJ 98381 36400 (197 m)
Unit and Station: No. 16 Elementary Flying Training School, RAF Burnaston, Derby, No. 51
    Group, Flying Training Command
Date: 2 July 1941
Crew: Pilot, survived
Leading Aircraftman Wells

Having judiciously cleared from a storm-swept Burnaston, pupil-pilot Leading Aircraftman Wells got lost, and with his fuel running low, made a precautionary landing near Draycott in the Moors. Although he struck a tree and crashed, badly damaging the aircraft, the accident was attributed to the weather, with no blame attaching to him.

Farming brothers Messrs John and Victor Brassington identified the site as 'the field with the bump.'

Visiting the Site
The site is not on a footpath, so permission must be obtained from Blakelow Farm.

14
Waterhouses

63 HUGHES 369E HELICOPTER, G-OABG (SEE FIGS 102–104)
Cauldon Lowe, south-west of Waterhouses

SK 07899 48036 (339 m)
Operator: private, ABGee (Toys) Limited, Belper
Date: 19 October 1996
Crew: pilot, killed
Mr Alan Bavis Godkin

Hughes 369E Helicopter G-OABG crashed in darkness and poor visibility at Cauldon Lowe, Staffordshire, exploding, catching fire, and killing its pilot-owner occupant, Mr Alan Godkin.

Mr Godkin had lifted off from Haydock Park (near St Helens, east of Liverpool) on his eleventh flight of the day. After a while he encountered rain, low cloud, and very poor visibility. However, he had 770 hours' experience with 585 on the Hughes Helicopter. Additionally, the machine had an automatic pilot and a moving-map, satellite-navigational aid. On the other hand, Mr Godkin had no instrument rating, while his night rating had lapsed.

He had been cleared to fly to his Matlock-area home, via Stoke, at a height of 'not above 1500 feet'. From Stoke, however, the politic safety height would have been 3,300 feet. Yet on contacting East Midlands Radar he was still flying at just 1,000 feet. The radar controller immediately recommended, 'I would climb to three thousand feet, at least.' Mr Godkin acknowledged, but only after a somewhat distracted pause.

After that the Air Traffic Control tape becomes increasingly poignant as Mr Godkin, a man of indomitable confidence, reveals a dawning awareness that he is in imminent danger of losing control.

'I'm in trouble, I've got a problem,' he had admitted from the outset. And now, having conceded, 'I'm completely blind so you tell me where to go,' he specifically asked to be taken to East Midlands. Only the radar controller soon realised that instead of following the headings passed, the helicopter appeared to be circling. In a series of mutually concerned exchanges, an increasingly introspective Mr Godkin confirmed that this was indeed the case, and that he had once again lost altitude.

Mr Godkin's perturbation was evident as he advised, 'Trying to climb again and I'm still losing my track …'. And only seconds later, with the on-board terrain-warning stridently sounding, he twice called, 'Bravo Golf, I'm in trouble …' After which the tape has only static ...

The Air Investigation Department inquiry established that after an erratic series of heading and height changes, the helicopter had fallen into a power-on, uncontrolled spiral and impacted heavily, nose down. It established too that the forward skids had buried themselves a yard deep which, with a debris spread of just ten yards, indicated a near-vertical impact.

Mr Derek Barleyman, of Cauldon Lowe, ran to help. 'I vaulted the wall into the field and ran towards the fire. But then I came upon the pilot, still in his seat, and realised that there was nothing I could do.'

Visiting the Site
The site is just yards from the A62, close to its junction with the B5417. But do not expect surface debris.

64 AVRO TUTOR
Winkhill, Waterhouses, Staffordshire

SK 07045 51038 (246 m)
Unit and Station: No. 2 Flying Training School, RAF Digby, Lincolnshire, No. 23 Group,
    Flying Training Command
Date: 13 December 1935
Crew: pilot, unhurt
Acting Pilot Officer Brian D. Sellick

On Friday 13 December 1935, pupil-pilot Acting Pilot Officer Brian Sellick became lost when a ground mist prevented him from picking out ground features. He made a successful precautionary landing, however, in a pasture outside Winkhill, Staffordshire.

Crowds of villagers, adults and schoolchildren, gathered around the machine so, having appointed a guard, Acting Pilot Officer Sellick telephoned Digby, and having persuaded his instructors that he had made the right decision in putting down, obtained permission to continue with his sortie. Accordingly, his machine was manhandled into place, and he duly took off, completing his flight – according to the *Leek Post and Times* account – without further mishap.

Clearly the confidence placed in this trainee pilot was justified, for when he retired in November 1966 it was as Group Captain Sellick, CBE, DSO, DFC and bar.

Mr Bill Phillips, of Tyre Farm, when asked about the precautionary landing, murmured, 'I was too shy to go and see it,' but indicated where the machine had touched down, pointing out that a stone wall had been removed since, and overhead electrical cables installed.

Not a crash, as such, but an incident typical of the era and of an area whose mists caused so many overflying aviators to become, as navigators euphemistically have it, 'uncertain of their position'. One recalls that during 1936–37 478 RAF bombers put down because they were lost!

Visiting the Site
The field is bounded by the A523 and Bentygrange Lane.

15

Newhaven

65 VICKERS WELLINGTON Mk 3 DF611 (SEE FIG 105)
Newhaven, Jug and Glass, A515

SK 15566 61643 (362 m) initial impact
SK 15664 61687 (350 m) terminal crash site
Unit and Station: No. 30 Operational Training Unit and Station (OTU), RAF Hixon, north-
  east of Stafford, No. 93 Group, Bomber Command
Date: 10 April 1943
Crew: Five, three killed, two injured
Sergeant Ronald Albert Jones, RAF Volunteer Reserve, pilot, killed
Sergeant John Scott Spencer, RAF, navigator, killed
Sergeant Gilbert Kenneth Parsons, RAFVR, bomb aimer, killed
Flight Sergeant R. J. Perrin, RAFVR, wireless operator, injured
Flight Sergeant John Douglas, RAFVR, air gunner, rear turret broke away, injured

On 10 April 1943 Sergeant Pilot Ronald Jones and his trainee crew were detailed for a pre-dawn infra-red bombing exercise in which a camera would show the accuracy of the bomb-release point. Despite an OTU regulation requiring all navigational route plans to be overseen before departure, and particularly in relation to safety height, 25 minutes after getting airborne Sergeant Jones flew his aircraft into ground elevated to 1,200 feet above sea level. The aircraft smashed through the drystone walls bordering the A515, halting with three men dead and two injured.

The court of inquiry submitted that the pilot had not told the navigator that he was trying to keep below cloud.

In 1982 Flight Sergeant John Douglas revisited the scene. Having survived both impact and fire because his rear turret had broken off, he had then completed a tour of operations, been awarded the Distinguished Flying Medal, and commissioned. Flight Sergeant Perrin, the wireless operator, however, had been killed on operations.

Visiting the Site
Parking is afforded by a lay-by on the A515, almost opposite the Jug and Glass pub, and although there is normally no surface evidence, metal does still emerge. It should be noted that the salvage team spilled debris between the crash site and the gate they utilised at SK 15534 61794. Also noteworthy is that the spent 0.303 cartridge cases which are commonplace over the 500 yards from the A515 to the High Peak Trail derive from army and Home Guard exercises, none being either belt-linked or heat-discharged.

66 GERMAN BOMBER (SEE FIG 106)
A515 Ashbourne–Buxton Road, Newhaven

SK 16499 60510 (350m)
Luftwaffe
1941

Mrs Beryl Rush (née Mellor) of Youlgreave, then of Friden, remembered this crash. 'We heard that a German bomber had crashed. So after Dad and some other Home Guard men had finished work, we walked up the road to The Newhaven [Hotel], then towards Buxton, and found it in the second field past the Newhaven Garage.'

Asked to differentiate between this and the crash of Wellington DF611 [above], which, on 10 April 1943, crashed two miles further up the Buxton road, Mrs Rush argued cogently, 'I was twelve when the German came down, and we moved to Bakewell in January 1943, so we'd been gone three months by the April.'

Only vague recollections emerged from canvassing very long-term Newhaven area residents, or from local press reports.

Visiting the Site
Lay-by parking is available on the A515 at Newhaven, opposite the junction with the A5012, but the site reveals no evidence.

16
Alsop-en-le-Dale

67 ARMSTRONG WHITWORTH WHITLEY Mk 5 EB338
(SEE FIG 107)

Tissington Trail, Alsop-en-le-Dale

SK 15023 55682 (293 m) terminal site
SK 15065 55715 295 m clipped wall and railway line
Unit and Station: No. 81 Operational Training Unit (OTU), RAF Tilstock, south of
    Whitchurch, Shropshire, No. 93 Group, Bomber Command
Date: 13 May 1943
Crew: six, one killed, five injured
Flying Officer Ernest James Bull, RAF Volunteer Reserve, OTU staff pilot, injured
Sergeant N. J. Prime, Royal New Zealand Air Force, pilot trainee, injured
Sergeant Gordon Belec, Royal Canadian Air Force, bomb aimer, killed
Sergeant Otty Spencer, RAFVR, wireless operator/air gunner, injured
Sergeant T. Kennedy, RAFVR, aircrew category unknown, injured
Sergeant E. F. Harris, RAFVR, aircrew category unknown, injured

Whitley EB338 was just thirty minutes into its sortie when its left-hand engine abruptly stopped. Its trainee pilot, Sergeant Prime, with under two hundred hours' flying, and just six on the Whitley, responded swiftly, and managed to re-start the failed engine only to have it cut once again. In concentrating on the troublesome engine, however, he allowed his speed to fall and was only able to regain a safe control speed by losing altitude.

Flying Officer Ernest Bull, the OTU staff instructor, was unable to offer effective help but did warn the crew of the impending crash. And moments later, having scraped an embanked railway line, the Whitley impacted heavily into a field. The bomb aimer, still at his station in the nose, was killed.

A technical examination showed that the malfunction had been caused by broken inlet-valve springs. However, the Air Officer Commanding had it recorded that the pilot had failed in his duty in not ordering the bomb-aimer to evacuate his only-too vulnerable station.

Mr Clem Edge, of Oxdales Farm, remembered watching the struggling aircraft. 'I thought, You'll not even make the main road. But he did. Then scraped the railway line, and came down in a field of oats two hundred yards or so up from the bridge – where the embankment dies down. It was not that badly smashed: still like an aeroplane.'

Another witness, Mr William Bunting, indicated where the aircraft had finished up. 'It was our field, but they kept us out for three days. And although the RAF let fuel all over the oats, Dad got compensation. They took the wings off, then carted the whole thing off on low loaders to Ashbourne.'

Visiting the Site
The site is equidistant between two Tissington Trail access areas on the A515, but no surface evidence remains.

17

Parwich

68 SUPERMARINE SPITFIRE Mk 22 PK488 (see fig 108)
Hilltop Farm, north of Parwich

SK 18832 55374 (286 m) touchdown
SK 18785 55155 (290 m) terminal site
Unit and Station: No. 502 (Ulster) Squadron, Royal Auxiliary Air Force, Reserve Command,
    RAF Aldergrove; detached to RAF Newton, Nottinghamshire
Date: 25 June 1949
Pilot: successfully forced-landed:
Flight Lieutenant A. MacDonald, Royal Auxiliary Air Force

When Flight Lieutenant MacDonald was scrambled from his exercise-detachment base at RAF Newton, near Nottingham, he was well aware that at combat settings his Spitfire virtually guzzled fuel. However, some time later he realised that he had not recently heard from ground control. With his fuel dwindling he also realised that, being over unfamiliar terrain, and despite an almost cloudless sky, he did not know where to turn for the nearest airfield. Accordingly, after deliberating, he decided he had no option but to make a precautionary landing. And clearly it was a timely decision, for having flown a visual pattern around a suitable-seeming field, made distinctive by a singular, cross-shaped wood, and near enough to both a farm and a village to ensure succour, his engine cut from lack of fuel at the very moment of touchdown.

The set-down was successful, but towards the final stages of his landing run Flight Lieutenant MacDonald encountered rough ground, causing the aircraft's undercarriage to collapse.

Initially it was recommended that a court of inquiry be held, but once it was found that the frequency-controlling crystal in the radio had failed this was overridden, the refreshingly pragmatic view being taken that it would have served no useful purpose, both pilot and fighter controllers being held as blameless.

Mr Charles Fearn, then a Parwich schoolboy, remembered the incident well. 'When word came that an aircraft had crashed at Hilltop Farm, me and my cousin, Dennis Evans, immediately set off up Parwich Hill. Then, as we came clear of the wood, there in the field between us and Hilltop Farm, facing uphill, was a hardly-damaged Spitfire. Our local policeman, PC Parker, was already in attendance and keeping the growing crowd back. He protested that the plane might explode at any moment but the pilot overruled him, and let us look around the cockpit and its controls.'

'The Spitfire,' his cousin, Mr Evans, remembered, 'wasn't smashed, just seemed to have flopped onto its belly. So we could easily see into the cockpit. There wasn't much chance of souvenirs, though.'

'Not with PC Parker's eagle eye on us,' Mr Fearn agreed, adding, 'The recovery team used a Thorneycroft-mounted Coles Crane and a Queen Mary trailer to recover the plane.'

Visiting the Site

There is no footpath serving the site, but parking might be obtained near Hilltop Farm. The field been constantly farmed ever since, so no trace of the incident remains.

69 DE HAVILLAND DH60G GIPSY MOTH (SEE FIG 109–110)
Mountain Ash Farm, north of Parwich

SK 18923 57389 (323 m) touchdown
SK 18743 57385 (326 m) terminal site
Owner: Privately owned, by RAF officer
Date: August 1928
Occupant: pilot, successfully forced-landed
Mr Norman Styche, not seriously hurt

Mr Asa Kirkham, of Ashbourne, was brought up at Mountain Ash Farm. 'It was in August 1928 that the Moth came down,' he remembered. 'The pilot, a Mr Norman Styche, was flying from Lincoln to Liverpool when he got lost. He decided to land, find out where he was, then get on his way again, so having circled the area a time or two, he chose our freshly-mown Long Meadow. Chary, however, of catching his wheels in the near wall he landed further along the field than he'd planned. He'd no brakes, only a skid on the rudder, and so when the slope began to take him to his left, he'd no way of straightening out.

'Dad and my brother had been watching him, but the moment the slope took him, Dad was alarmed. "The bugger's going to crash into my hay stack," he shouted, and both of them began to run. The pilot, however, had realised that he was far more likely to crash into the adjacent stone barn. So next thing, they saw him leaping from the cockpit and letting the plane carry on. In fact, just short of both barn and stacked hay, it hit the drystone wall and tipped over it, the wooden propeller breaking off as it hit the ground on the far side, the tail rearing straight up. At first Dad was more concerned over the petrol catching fire and destroying his hay, but when nothing happened, he turned his attention to the pilot. To find that the tail had banged his head as it passed him, leaving him a bit dazed and headachey.'

Mr Kirkham smiled. 'Anyway, they got him back to Mountain Ash, and mother took care of his head. And a little later Dad drove him into Parwich, to a phone. After which he spent the night with Mr Etches, at Royston Grange Farm.' Mr Kirkham paused to reflect. 'Under his overalls he was dressed in ordinary clothes. But next day an Air Ministry vehicle with a driver and two mechanics bumped their way over to the plane, loaded the body, then tucked the wings down the side.' He smiled again. 'But we'd laid claim to one of the rod-like struts that held the wings up above the cockpit, so Dad fitted it with a brass knob and a ferrule and made a walking-stick of it.'

Visiting the Site

The site is on private land on Mountain Ash Farm, Parwich Lane, but though wall and barn remain there is nothing to show of this incident. A footpath crosses the landing run, however, and unlike the 1928 incumbent the present owner does not tether a bad-tempered bull by one of the stiles to deter walkers.

70 BELL B206B JET RANGER Mᴋ 3 HELICOPTER G-NORM (see fig 111)

Brook Close Farm, Parwich

SK 18489 54104 (214 m)
Operator: Norman Bailey, Southampton
Date: 13 May 1984
Occupants: two pilots, operating pilot killed
Major Simon Hugh Codman Marriot, Greenjackets (Rifle Regiment)
Mr Peter Bradley Banks, killed

Mr Robert Shields, of Parwich Hall, had arranged to have Major Simon Marriot, a pilot with some 3,000 flying hours, carry out a helicopter survey of his Longcliffe holdings. With the task completed, Major Marriot landed at Brook Close Farm. Mr Shields disembarked, and Major Marriot handed control to Mr Peter Banks, a private pilot with 23 hours on Jet Rangers but under 200 hours total experience. Meanwhile, Mr Shields had offered a flight to haulage contractor Mr Frank Dale.

'But,' Mr Dale said, 'they were too low on fuel. So they lifted off without me. Only they backed slightly.' He indicated the ridge-and-furrow undulations of the field, the tops – 'launts' or 'balks' – a full eighteen inches above the furrows. 'A skid hit a launt, and the helicopter heeled over.' He paused. 'One of the blades broke off and a two-foot piece came flying over our heads to land down at Staines Cottage, at the foot of the hill. But the rest smashed back into the right-hand side of the machine. The Major scrambled clear but the other pilot was killed instantly.'

He eyed the ground. 'At the time we didn't know that, of course. The engine was still howling away, the tail rotor was spinning wildly, and fuel was pouring out, worrying us that the whole thing would catch fire. But while Robert and I lifted up the helicopter, Reg and the Major managed to reach in and drag Mr Banks clear.'

No mean effort, and what a risk! Yet, 'What else could you do?' Mr Dale posed stolidly.

On considering the site, the investigators identified several problems: the sloping ground, the large furrows, and the necessity to make a turn into wind immediately after lift off. They found that when the skid touched the ground it imparted a rolling motion to the rotors which, in turn, diminished the lateral control and faced the relatively inexperienced pilot with the potentially catastrophic condition known as dynamic rollover. Just the same, they concluded that the take-off should have been well within Mr Banks' capabilities.

Major Marriot, speaking from his subsequently enhanced experience of over 7,000 hours, remembered, 'I'd looked down at the map, when I realised that a correcting input had become necessary. But before I could assume control the aft end of a skid had hit the ground and we had a dynamic rollover on our hands. It was the work of an instant. And a bitter lesson learnt.'

Visiting the Site
No surface evidence remains, and the site is on private ground at Brook Close Farm. The Limestone Way, though, is just one field distant, the view across Parwich to Parwich Hill with its singular cross-shaped wood being well worth the climb.

18

Aldwark

71 STINSON SR-10 RELIANT W7982 (SEE FIGS 112–113)
Slipper Low, Tithe Farm, Aldwark

SK 22024 56491 (343 m) Site derived by early investigators
SK 22018 57181 (343 m) Site derived from the RAF accident report summary
Unit and Station: No. 1 Camouflage Unit, RAF Bicester, No. 11 Group, Fighter Command
Date: 15 April 1941
Crew: pilot and two passengers, uninjured:
Sergeant Verney-Cave, pilot
Passengers, unidentified

Being easy to handle and having a built-in stability that enabled it to recover 'hands-off' from any inadvertent stall, the Stinson Reliant 'Gullwing' four- to five-seater was well suited to contact flying. However, like all aircraft, it demanded respect.

Sergeant Verney-Cave had a healthy enough 1,700 hours' total flying experience and 150 hours solo on Reliants, so when his engine gave trouble and he crashed on carrying out a forced-landing at Slipper Low, the court of inquiry found that he had mishandled both the engine problem and the landing.

The preferred location is that determined by early enthusiast investigators. This differs from the distance and bearing given by the RAF accident-report summary – rarely accurate in this detail

– which puts it on the north-western slope of Slipper Low. Regrettably, no local knowledge of the incident could be traced.

Visiting the Site
The preferred site, reached from a farm track leading off Moor Lane – the Longcliffe-Elton Road – shows no evidence of the incident. Nor does the RAF-derived location.

19
Bakewell

72 VICKERS WELLINGTON 1C DV678 (SEE FIGS 114–115)
Lindup Low, Chatsworth Park

SK 25436 69112 (161 m)
Unit and Station: No. 14 Operational Training Unit, RAF Cottesmore, 6 miles north-east of
    Oakham, No. 92 Group, Bomber Command
Date: 11 June 1943
Crew: three, all slightly injured
Flying Officer Leo Braham Patkin, Royal Australian Air Force, pilot
Two other crew members, unidentified

Flying Officer Leo Patkin was flying at 6,500 feet when both engines began to splutter. Judging it politic to set the machine down, he belly-landed in Chatsworth Park, beside the road at the brow of Lindup Low. All three occupants were injured, one suffering facial lacerations.

Mr Charles Roose, whose family were occupying the singular walled-about Keeper's Cottage – and who, in late 1944, was accepted for aircrew – arrived at the scene within minutes. 'It had come over Beeley', he recounted, 'and appeared virtually intact, although one of the crew had taken position on the floor and his face actually came into contact with the ground. As for the aircraft, just hours later Queen Mary trailers arrived, and it was gone by that afternoon.' He smiled. 'And what little there was left, us lads made short work of.'

The court of inquiry observed that with 6,500 feet in hand, Flying Officer Patkin should have been able to fly onwards to an airfield. His station commander, however, argued that since then Flying Officer Patkin had experienced another engine failure and made a successful landing. Accordingly, no disciplinary action was taken.

Flying Officer Patkin, later flight lieutenant, joined No. 467 Squadron but was killed on 1 January 1944 when his Lancaster (LM372) was shot down near Celle while raiding Berlin.

Visiting the Site
The Chatsworth Park road ascending from Carlton Lees car park passes the site. That no surface evidence remains is compensated for by the varied walks offered by the Chatsworth grounds.

20
Youlgreave

73 VICKERS WELLINGTON Mκ 1C L7811 (SEE FIGS 116–117)
Conksbury Bridge, Youlgreave

SK 21099 65770 (146 m)

Unit and Station: No. 149 Squadron, RAF Mildenhall, south-east of Ely, No. 3 Group, Bomber
   Command

Date: 12 February 1941

Crew: six, successfully baled out

Sergeant Turner, pilot

Sergeant Campbell, second pilot

Sergeant McKnight, observer/bomb aimer

Sergeant Pates, wireless operator/air gunner, sprained ankle

Sergeant Piper, air gunner

Sergeant Rae, air gunner

Having raided Bremen, Sergeant Turner's crew became lost above cloud. Why they were unable
to get aid is not known, but as the fuel dwindled Sergeant Turner showed eminent sense in
deciding to abandon rather than to descend blindly through cloud. The forsaken Wellington
spiralled into a slope in Lathkill Dale, just upstream from Conksbury Bridge, and over a hundred
miles from its Cambridgeshire base.

   One crew member landed in a tree at Swiss Cottage, in Chatsworth Park, another in a field
near Sheldon, a third by Beeley Bridge, and a fourth in Park Lane, Rowsley. Sergeant McKnight,
however, a Scot, knocked at Upper Haddon's Manor Farm Cottage and was taken to the Home
Guard picquet at the post office, only to find that his accent led to levelled rifles. Whether the
airman truly found the situation fraught is not known but when another of the crew arrived he
instantly threw his arms around him.

   Mr Joe Oldfield, of Upper Haddon, was able to indicate where the aircraft fell, while Mrs
Joan Dale, of Youlgreave, produced a ring made from its perspex by her brother, a Halifax flight
engineer on leave from operations: the first instance of this 'cottage industry' encountered!

Visiting the Site
There is adequate parking in the Conksbury Bridge area, the site lying just 185 yards upstream
along the Lathkill footpath. Metal exists on both sides of the path and in the river, but surface
debris is rare. On the other hand, from here, the whole of Lathkill awaits the discerning walker.

Miles Master Mk 3 W8840, Bottom House
See page 86

89. Mr Fred Gee standing on the impact point of Master W8840.

90. (Inset) Miles Master.

Douglas C-53 Skytrooper, Ossom's Hill
See page 97

91. Mr Arthur Coates and the wall he rebuilt at the impact site.

92. (Inset) Douglas C-53D Skytrooper.

Vickers Wellington Mk 3 Z1566, Sheldon Farm
See page 98

93. The crash site.

94. To the left, the old stone barn where the bodies from Wellington Z1566 were laid out ...

Consolidated B-24 Liberator, Brown Edge
See page 99

95. The terminal site, from the drystone wall where the crew of 42-52625 sheltered.

De Havilland Mosquito KB206, Cheddleton Heath
See page 101

96. The impact point of the fuselage of Mosquito KB206, looking towards Cheddleton Heath Road.

97. Mr Isaac Hudson standing on the track (since excavated) where the pilot of KB206 fell.

*Republic P-47 Thunderbolt,
Greenway Hall
See page 102*

98. The crash site in late 2011.

99. (Inset) Debris from Thunderbolt 42-74728 in 2012.

100. Above Steel House Farm, where the mortally injured pilot of 42-74728 landed.

English Electric Canberra B Mk 2 WH669, Dilhorne
See page 103

101. The impact area of Canberra WH669, with debris scraps.

*Hughes Helicopter G-OABG,
Cauldron Lowe
See page 105*

Right: **102.** Hughes
Helicopter G-OABG.

Below: **103.** The scene of
the crash of G-OABG, in
thick fog.

Bottom: **104.** Investigators
at the scene of the crash.

Vickers Wellington Mk 3 DF611,
Jug and Glass
See page 107

Above: **105.** The site of the
crash of Wellington DF611.

German bomber, Newhaven
See page 108

Left: **106.** Where the German
aircraft is thought to have
landed, Newhaven.

Armstrong Whitworth Whitley Mk 5 EB338, Tissington Trail
See page 108

Right: **107.** Mr William Bunting at the impact point on the railway of Whitley EB338; the terminal site is behind the inquisitive cow.

Supermarine Spitfire PK488, Hilltop Farm
See page 109

108. Looking along the landing run at Hill Farm.

De Havilland DH60G Gypsy Moth, Mountain Ash Farm
See page 110

109. The touch-down site of the Gypsy Moth at Mountain Ash Farm.

110. (Inset) The site of the final impact.

Bell B206B Jet Ranger Mk 3 Helicopter G-NORM, Brook Close Farm
See page 111

111. Mr Frank Dale, almost a passenger on G-NORM, at the crash site.

Stinson Reliant W7982, Slipper Low
See page 112

Below: **112.** The site where Reliant W7982 crashed.

113. (Inset) The crash site of W7982, derived from the RAF crash report summary.

Vickers Wellington Mk 1C DV678, Chatsworth
See page 113

114. The terminal impact site of Wellington DV678, Lindup Low.

115. (Inset) Belted and corroded, 0.303 inch calibre ammunition removed from the site.

Vickers Wellington Mk 1C L7811, Conksbury Bridge See page 114

Above: **116.** The location of the crash of Wellington L7811, walking upstream from Conksbury Bridge. The impact site is upslope to the right.

Left: **117.** The first evidence of L7811 found, near the river's edge.

Matlock

74 BRISTOL FIGHTER Mк 3 J8432
Matlock Moor, adjacent to Matlock Golf Course

SK 31183 62224 (222 m)
Unit and Station: No. 5 Flying Training School, RAF Sealand, near Chester, Headquarters
  Inland Area
Date: 16 July 1928
Crew: pupil pilot, superficial injuries
Pilot Officer Charles Lilburn Myers

Pilot Officer Charles Myers, a pupil on 'A' (Army Co-operation) Flight of the Advanced Squadron of No. 5 Flying Training School, became lost on a cross-country flight. He found himself over a moderately sized town, but was unable to locate himself. Sensibly, therefore, he decided to put down and determine his whereabouts. Selecting an area to the north-east of the town, he touched down, and aided by the braking effect of the tail skid on the long grass, soon came to a halt; to find people already running to the spot.

In fact, he had landed in the Cuckoostone Valley, in Derbyshire, touching down upslope of what was to become the eleventh green of the Matlock Golf Club – and upslope, too, of the eponymous Cuckoo Stone.

As *The Matlock Visitor (incorporating the Matlock Guardian and List of Visitors)* reported, 'At about 11 am on Monday morning a large RAF plane was noticed circling Matlock. It then dipped behind a hill in the direction of the golf course'.

Mr Norman Travis, a club member, recorded, 'We were soon able to set the pilot's mind at rest regarding his whereabouts. Then, on his instructions, we swung the machine around to enable him to get airborne once again.'

Significantly, there is no mention of Pilot Officer Myers taxying back to his touchdown point! Which implies that he had either landed downwind, or intended to take-off downwind. In either event, his take-off run was certainly slightly uphill. Only Pilot Officer Myers made another fundamental error.

'There was a fair distance before the walls of Martin's Path,' noted a bystander, 'but he tried to take off through mowing grass. So although he managed to lift, he couldn't clear the wall, and smashed over into the path.'

A fair assessment, for the high, unmown grass dragging at the wheels prevented even the 275 horsepower of the Rolls-Royce Falcon engine from giving the machine adequate flying speed. Accordingly, it impacted into one of the path-bordering drystone walls, and flipped ignominiously into the lane beyond. Pilot Officer Myers suffered only superficial injuries.

The badly damaged aircraft was left in the lane for some days before being recovered, but it was to be 1929 before it was transferred to the Home Aircraft Depot at RAF Henlow.

The accident was attributed to misadventure due to lack of experience. And on 18 September 1928, having gained his wings, Pilot Officer Myers was posted to No. 28 Squadron, in India. But just two months later, on 6 November 1928, he was killed while engaged on army co-operation duties on the turbulent North-West Frontier.

Visiting the Site

The crash site, served by several fine footpaths, all of which can be accessed from the A632, is on the wall-bordered Martin's Path. There is no trace, however, of the incident.

75 MILES MAGISTER Mᴋ 1 N3811 (sᴇᴇ ꜰɪɢ 118)
Snitterton, west of Matlock

SK 27830 60498 (74 m)
Unit and Station: No. 16 Elementary Flying Training School, RAF Burnaston, Derby, No. 51
    Group, Flying Training Command
Date: 31 July 1940
Crew: pilot, uninjured:
Leading Aircraftman K. P. Glassborow

When Leading Aircraftman K. P. Glassborow, a pupil pilot with under fifty hours of flying experience, lost himself during a general-handling detail, he decided to make a precautionary landing. Most fields that presented themselves were obstructed by ditches and 'anti-invasion' posts – vertical poles intended to deter landings by German troop-transporting aircraft. The one he chose, however, though free of both obstacles, had a downhill slope that caused him to overrun into a drystone wall.

Mr Harold Petts, of Snitterton, pinpointed the location. 'It finished up in the first of Major Bagshaw's fields, just beyond Snitterton Hall, and facing downhill. The pilot evidently decided to land near a big house which was likely to have a telephone but ran into what was then a wall.'

An innocuous enough set-down, then. Although not so innocuous to Leading Aircraftman Glassborow, who had to explain his aircraft's presence in a field some 23 miles from Burnaston. Undoubtedly, however, with elementary flying training being forced through at an unprecedented rate, the incident would have been benignly viewed.

Visiting the Site

The site is off the Snitterton Road, to the west of Matlock, and has two public footpaths passing through it. The set-down, however, has left no trace.

76 MILES MAGISTER
Upper Town, Bonsall

SK 27200 58480 (281 m)
Unit and Station: No. 16 Elementary Flying Training School, RAF Burnaston, Derby, No. 51
    Group, Flying Training Command
Date: 1940
Crew: pilot, unidentified, unhurt

In 1940 a Magister which became lost on a training exercise and ran short of fuel forced-landed on a hillside at Upper Town, Bonsall, just west of Matlock. Although it caused a stir in the village at the time the incident was innocuous enough, for after the authorities arrived, the machine was refuelled and took off again, the pilot occupying the front seat, although the type could be flown solo from either seat.

Mr Lewis Pearson, of Bonsall, went to see the machine. 'The pilot who put the Magister down was a big, tall chap,' he remembered, 'yet that didn't deter Mrs Rains, from Upper Town Farm. For as he dropped the side hatch and climbed out, she ran down the field with a pitchfork shouting, "I'll see you off, you Jerry, you!" But that got straightened out. And after refuelling, he took off again, downhill, and without turning around.'

Visiting the Site

The field, unsurprisingly enough, shows no sign of its erstwhile visitor, but as it is traversed at its south-western end, nearest Upper Town, by a public footpath, the incident, although in no sense a crash, may be of interest to the passing walker.

77 DE HAVILLAND DH82A TIGER MOTH BB811 (SEE FIG 119)
Carr Lane, Dethick, Matlock

SK 32555 58876 (207 m)
Unit and Station: RAF No. 20 Elementary Flying Training School, RAF Yeadon (Bradford),
    Flying Training Command
Date: 17 December 1941
Crew: pilot, unhurt:
Leading Aircraftman Frederick Stanley Eastwell

When pupil pilot Leading Aircraftman Frederick Eastwell became lost he decided to set down while he still had fuel. Failing to touch down early enough, however, and with the Tiger Moth having no brakes, he overran, striking a drystone wall. The aircraft immediately burst into flames but LAC Eastwood jumped clear.

The inquiry put this mishap down to inexperience – LAC Eastwell had just 14 hours solo – and he went on to captain Halifaxes in No. 51 Squadron. On 2 March 1945, however, as Flying Officer Eastwell, he was shot down and killed over Belgium.

Visiting the Site

The site is along Carr Lane (accessed from the A615), near its junction with Green Lane.

78 MILES MAGISTER L8277 (SEE FIG 120)
Hollybush Farm, Moorwood Moor, South Wingfield, Alfreton

SK 35845 56754 (166 m) area of successful landing run
SK 35915 56689 (157 m) area of impact into hedge on attempting take-off
Unit and Station: No. 16 Elementary Flying Training School, RAF Burnaston (Derby), No. 51
    Group, Flying Training Command
Date: mid-1942
Crew: two, both uninjured
Sergeant Pilot Louis
Unidentified passenger

After landing in a field to ascertain his position, Sergeant Pilot Louis, a staff pilot at RAF
Burnaston, failed to allow for the unprepared surface and on take-off was unable to gain flying
speed, crashing through the boundary hedge and seriously damaging the Magister.

Mrs Jean Ludlam, of Ludlam's Farm, South Wingfield, remembered how she heard about the
incident. 'As a newly-wed I was working part-time in Woolworths at Alfreton when someone
told me that a German plane had come down near our place. Of course, knowing I'd have to walk
home across the fields, I was worried about running into a German. When I left the bus I could
see a wing of the plane stuck up in the air in Hollybush Farm's Ten-Acre Field, so I was relieved
on getting indoors to find Pamela Jane, my mother-in-law, feeding seven or eight soldiers. They
guarded the plane overnight, then the RAF took it off in long trailers.'

Intriguingly, the RAF field investigators located this incident at 'Maud' instead of 'Moorwood'!
Then again, the authoritative *Air Britain* records show that L8277 never had an accident.

Visiting the Site
Farming was barely interrupted by the set-down, so no trace exists.

79 AVRO ANSON, Mk 2 (SEE FIG 121)
Mount Pleasant Farm, Wessington, Alfreton

SK 38378 58162 (111 m) impact area, farm track
SK 38145 58112 (115 m) terminal area, top field
Unit and Station: Flying Training Command
Date: mid-1943
Crew: occupants, unidentified, one slightly injured

The Avro Anson was not all that happy on one engine, so when the pilot of this one suffered an engine failure he aimed to carry out a forced-landing on a field beside Mount Pleasant Farm, at Wessington. As it was, he overshot the mark, struck the farm drive, then bounced, and crashed through a hedge into the field beyond. The occupants survived, and although the aircraft was substantially damaged it was soon back in service again.

Mr Alan Jerome was twelve at the time. 'The plane,' he recalled, 'came from the Derby direction. It was making such a noise! And only skimming the trees. Then, as it came to Massey's Farm it disappeared. Then it bumped, came up again – twenty feet or so, into the air, it seemed – then hit again quite a way further on.'

As Mrs Eileen Newton, of The Farm, Lea, recalled, 'I was about twelve and at school at Brackenfield when we went to see the crashed plane. It was all smashed but they said nobody had been killed, only the pilot had broken his ankle …'

Visiting the Site

The incident occurred on private land and although the field layout has not changed since, authorised searches turned up no physical evidence of the crash.

23
Ashbourne (North)

80 ARMSTRONG WHITWORTH ALBEMARLE V1604 (SEE FIGS 122–123)

Bradley Pastures, Ashbourne

SK 22385 47074 (176 m)
Unit and Station: No. 42 Operational Training Unit, RAF Ashbourne, No. 38 (Airborne Force) Group, Allied Expeditionary Air Force
Date: 12 March 1944
Crew: five, all killed:
Flying Officer James Duncan MacTavish Baillie, pilot
Flying Officer Willebrodus Maria Antoine Van Leemputten, navigator
Sergeant Norman White, wireless operator/air gunner
Flight Sergeant Basil Herbert Symes, air gunner
Sergeant James Robertson Graham, air gunner

In early 1944, with the invasion of Europe imminent, one of the pressing needs was to train crews for paratroop-dropping duties, the Albemarle task falling upon No. 42 Operational Training Unit (OTU) at RAF Ashbourne. But after Albemarle V1604 was lost the subsequent inquiry threw into stark relief the strain imposed on the pilot-training organisation.

It is clear that as the trainee crew neared Ashbourne they grew uncertain of their position, for at one stage the pilot called for assistance from the 'Darky' get-you-home organisation. Perhaps that helped, for the next contact was when he called Ashbourne for 'Floods'. Only notwithstanding that the flood-lighting switch was thrown at once, the aircraft impacted into a field at Bradley Pastures Farm, just two miles from the airfield, disintegrating and burning, and killing all the crew.

The court of inquiry had an unenviable task, but their remit allowed no pulling of punches. While fully appreciative of the mental pressure that threatens the tyro pilot when low cloud, poor visibility, darkness, and seat-of-the-pants-certainty combine to override the assurance the flight instruments are endeavouring to impart, they used the word 'panic' to describe this hapless pilot's response.

It was to be left to the unit's commanding officer to baldly declare that the appointment of a below-average pilot to paratroop-dropping training should never have been made; a declaration upheld by higher authority, who instituted a thorough review of the proficiency of those pilots sent to such duties.

Brothers Ron and Tom Archer remembered the trauma of that night. 'When we got to the scene we realised that there would be no survivors. There was wreckage everywhere, a great crater, with just the tail sticking out, and fire: later we had to restore a full thirty yards of the hedge. And there were body parts strewn all over. In fact, it traumatised us, Dad too, for years to come.'

Their cousin, Mr Ray Archer, first visited 'Albemarle Field' when the RAF salvage team was clearing the wreckage. 'It was apparent,' he recalled, 'that when a wing struck, the machine had been dragged into the ground. Also, the fact that the engines were so far away, each gouging its own crater, showed it had been going at speed.'

Visiting the Site

The field, off the A517, remains private property but authorised investigations furnished adequate proof of the site. There is no surface evidence, however.

81 ARMSTRONG WHITWORTH ALBEMARLE P1463 (SEE FIG 124)
Wigber Low, Bradbourne, near Ashbourne

SK 20269 52016 (165 m) main structure over hedge, tail in ditch
SK 20232 52005 (178 m) pilot, through the top wall
SK 20127 52130 (150 m) wheel, near stream.
Unit and Station: No. 42 Operational Training Unit and Station (OTU), RAF Ashbourne, No. 38 (Airborne Force) Group, Allied Expeditionary Air Force
Date: 30 March 1944
Crew: four, all killed
Pilot Officer Douglas Reginald Revitt, RAF Volunteer Reserve, pilot
Flying Officer Eric Matthew Montagu O'Connor, Royal Australian Air Force, pilot
Flight Sergeant Samuel Morrison, trainee pilot
Sergeant Kenneth George Bruce Scammell, wireless operator/air gunner

Minutes after getting airborne from Ashbourne, OTU instructor Pilot Officer Douglas Revitt's Albemarle, now festooned with lengths of power cables, dived into the lower slopes of Wigber Low, near Bradbourne, and exploded in flames, killing all four occupants.

It was clear to the investigators that the operating pilots had been unable to gain height, for the power cables, just north of Bank Top Farm, were at 800 feet above sea level; that is, only some 200 feet higher than Ashbourne airfield. It was equally evident that they had already been in trouble before striking, for they had turned back towards Ashbourne.

The investigators postulated that the flaps had been raised too early, so robbing the wings of much-needed lift and committing the aircraft to semi-stalled flight at a fatally low level. However, they were never able to determine a definite cause for the accident.

Mr John Myers, incumbent of Bradbourne Mill, but then aged fifteen, remembered being awoken by an unexplained brilliance lighting up Rookery Field. 'Until the police rang from Ashbourne and asked if dad knew anything about an aeroplane that had crashed.'

The aircraft had finished up across a ditched hedge running up the hill, its tail on one side, nose on the other, and the whole ablaze, with crackling ammunition. Would-be rescuers were quickly on the scene. But nothing could aid the occupants.

Only there were elements of black comedy. So that, emerging from the Mill, John Myers was held back and bade, 'Listen – that hissing's a bomb about to go off,' only to see an aircraft wheel with air escaping from its punctured tyre.

And when a late arrival asked mildly, 'What about that chap up there?' and admitted to having checked the identity discs of the pilot he had found thrown clear of the fire and through a drystone wall, he was soundly berated by both police and fire service for 'interfering with evidence'.

As for the local Air Raid Precaution (ARP) warden, two maiden ladies from the village roused him in mid-morning next day. 'We were banging at your door when that aeroplane crashed last night,' they charged, 'and couldn't wake you.'

'Well,' he frowned, 'I was flat out. I'd been to ARP training at Ashbourne. But don't be so soft – what plane?'

Later that day the young John Myers was set to the task of carting the wreckage to the road, the steepness of the slope obliging him to change from horse and cart to a lime-spreading sledge. As he says, 'Back then there was no counselling, or post-traumatic shock, just early-morning milking, and cows waiting to be fed.'

Visiting the Site

The terminal crash site is on private ground at Bradbourne Mill, on the B5056, but there is no evidence of the crash, only a pasture edged with a barbed-wire-lined hedge. From the terminal site Haven Hill hides the power cables on Bank Top.

82 EUROPA G-KWIP (SEE FIGS 125–126)
Holly Meadow Farm, Bradley, Ashbourne

SK 23050 44822 (162 m)
Operator: private owner
Date: 12 March, 2000
Occupants: two, both seriously injured
Mr Graham Singleton, pilot
Mr Isaac Porat, passenger

Aircraft engineer and private pilot Mr Graham Singleton planned to fly Europa G-KWIP to Tatenhill Aerodrome, in Staffordshire. However, in the course of taking off from Mr Tom Lawton's strip at Holly Meadow Farm, Bradley, the Europa's engine lost power, after which the aircraft stalled into the ground, grievously injuring both occupants.

Mr Singleton had some 500 hours' flying experience, including 250 on type, and was also an approved inspector for the Private Flying Association. As such, he had played a major role in building G-KWIP which, when it crashed, had flown some 210 hours.

One of the officially approved modifications carried out during the building had involved diluting the water-glycol mixture for the engine's cooling system. Besides this, Mr Singleton had been collaborating with the passenger, Mr Isaac Porat, a university professor and a specialist in the electronics and computer fields, in developing a Light-Aircraft Glass Cockpit (LAGC) system which would, in essence, supplement the normal instruments with a sophisticated 'plug-in' computer-based display. This project had already proved itself during three hours of flying and it was now to be inspected at Tatenhill.

Testifying to the Aircraft Accident Investigation Bureau (AAIB), Mr Jonathan Tye, of Holloway, formerly the RAF's Vulcan display pilot, reported that before flight the Europa's engine had been heard to stop – at that stage witnesses were unsighted by a dip in the ground – only restarting after a considerable delay. He reported, too, a far more protracted delay, presumably as the instrumentation computer was being set up. Eventually, however, the aircraft had lifted into sight. 'As the Europa took off I saw a stream of smoke coming from the engine bay. The aircraft didn't seem able to climb any higher than about 50 feet. Graham was struggling at the controls, but he couldn't stop it diving into a ploughed field.'

The AAIB inspectors established that when the loss of power occurred the aircraft began 'a gentle turn to the left', noting though, that, despite the power loss, 'the aircraft remained in the same nose up take-off attitude' as it commenced this turn, only for the engine to pick up. By which time, however, the left wing had dropped, with the nose following in an incipient spin that took the aircraft heavily into the ground.

The AAIB found that the loss of engine power was probably due to an increase in engine temperature during the lengthy delay on the ground. As a noted engineer, however, Mr Singleton was able to show a flaw in the technicalities, leading to the AAIB – in what has to be a very rare move – issuing an addendum to their report.

Visiting the Site
As might be expected, with the crash investigated so minutely, nothing is to be seen at the site, which is on private farmland and relatively remote from public footpaths.

83 ARMSTRONG WHITWORTH WHITLEY (SEE FIG 127)
Holly Meadow Farm, Bradley, Ashbourne

SK 23307 44552 (146 m)
Unit and Station: No 42 Operational Training Unit, RAF Ashbourne, No. 38 Group
Date: summer, 1943

Mr Tom Lawton, of Holly Meadow Farm, remembered where this training Whitley from RAF Ashbourne came down. 'I was brought across to see it but the guard kept us well back. Even so, Joe Moss, the farmer then, was able to ladle up petrol from the ditch.'

Visiting the Site
The site yielded no physical evidence.

84 ARMSTRONG WHITWORTH WHITLEY (SEE FIG 128)
Hole in the Wall, Bradley

SK 21116 45906 (186 m) initial impact
SK 21295 46067 (195 m) terminal point
Unit and Station: RAF Ashbourne, No. 42 Operational Training Unit, No. 70 Group, Air
   Defence Great Britain Command (Fighter Command).
Date: 25 May 1944
Crew: four, unhurt
Flying Officer Kelham, Operational Training Unit, pilot instructor
Flight Lieutenant Finn, pilot
Two others, unidentified
Flying Officer Kelham was monitoring his trainee, Flight Lieutenant Finn, on a local-flying
detail when, moments after lift-off, their port engine failed.

The immediate need was to overcome the pull towards the failed engine, which, if not counteracted,
would have rolled them into the ground. At the same time it was necessary to maintain a minimum
control speed. But with the right-hand engine already at full power, this would have meant
lowering the nose. Only the aircraft did that for itself, falling into what both pilots reported as 'an
uncontrollable dive'. They did, however, manage to check the descent, but struck the ground, then a
tree, before careering across a field. None of the four crew members was hurt.

The drag of the failed propeller had taken the aircraft off to the left, and just as well, for initially
it had been heading towards New Park Farm, then the home of the Wigley family. As Mrs Hilda
Page (née Wigley) remembered, 'Mother saw the plane through the kitchen window, and cried
out, for it looked as if it was going to fly straight into the house. So I ran upstairs and grabbed
my baby son. But by then it had swung off to our right.' Mrs Page paused, then smiled. 'Dad and
I ran across – I can see it now, tilted over onto one wheel –, but they were all getting out. Then
one of them said, "To think it's my twenty-first today!"'

Farmer Mr Ron Archer was early at the scene. 'First,' he said, 'it decapitated two cows, then it
hit an oak, which it gouged its way across the field, stopping about thirty yards short of the hedge.'
He reflected. 'It wasn't all that badly damaged, although it took them some time to clear.'

Visiting the Site
Footpaths crossing Bradley Moor bracket the crash site, but, though the oak shows where a major
branch was torn off, farming only stopped during the recovery operation. By early 2012, even the
distant runway had largely been gouged up.

85 MILES MAGISTER MK 1 T9823 (SEE FIG 129)
Hallfield Farm, south of Kniveton, Ashbourne

SK 22037 48195 (222 m)
Unit and Station: No. 16 Elementary Flying Training School, RAF Burnaston, Derby, No. 51
   Group, Flying Training Command
Date: 5 December 1941
Crew: pilot, killed
Pilot Officer Victor Harry Saunders, RAF Volunteer Reserve, pilot

Newly fledged Pilot Officer Victor Saunders was killed when, encountering cloudy conditions and poor visibility, he struck high ground at Hallfield Farm, to the north-east of Ashbourne.

The court of inquiry found that he had made an error of judgement in not turning back into clearer air and known lower ground, the Air Officer Commanding additionally pointing to inadequacies in pre-flight preparations. Certainly, Pilot Officer Saunders had reached one of several recognised danger periods in a pilot's career when, imbued with all the confidence imparted by gaining one's wings, an element of 'press-on' might take over from the meticulous attention to safety called for in the closely-monitored pre-Wings training days.

Visiting the Site

A knot of footpaths serve the area but there is nothing to show of the crash, near a dew pond to the east of this private property. Local farmer Mr Ray Archer, however, remembered, 'For years I kept a foot-long section of the wooden propeller as a souvenir ...'

86 ARMSTRONG WHITWORTH WHITLEY EB337 (SEE FIG 130)
Crowtrees Farm, Bradley

SK 22690 46530 (200 m)
Unit and Station: RAF Ashbourne, No. 42 Operational Training Unit, No. 70 Group, Air Defence Great Britain Command (Fighter Command)
Date: 22 November 1944
Crew: probably six, unhurt
Flying Officer Only, pilot, OTU instructor
Remainder of crew unidentified

Flying Officer Only was engaged in circuit work with a trainee crew when, lined-up just two miles from the runway and with a good 750 feet in hand, he suffered an engine malfunction that turned the aircraft to the right. Either the engine had failed and the propeller had refused to feather, setting up an enormous drag instead, or it had begun to overspeed, whirling around at a seemingly ever-increasing rate, threatening to tear the engine from its mounting, but almost at once rendering the aircraft virtually uncontrollable.

By the time Flying Officer Only was able to assume command and begin to contain the situation, the right turn had brought into view a sizeable field of rye. Powerless to prevent the aircraft descending, he nursed it down, running the length of the field and halting just yards before the far hedge.

Mr Tom Archer, a fifteen-year-old living at nearby Bradley Pastures Farm, was an early visitor. 'The plane was facing east,' he recalled, 'away from Ashbourne, and seemed totally undamaged. But by the next night nothing was left, just the gaps in the hedge which the RAF had cut for their Queen Marys.' He laughed. 'Of course, the field was full of anti-invasion poles, but he'd managed to miss every one of them. So it would be nice to think he got at least a pat on the back.'

Visiting the Site

The roadside field, beside the A517, north of Bradley, retains the same proportions as it did then, but there is nothing to see of the incident.

87 ARMSTRONG WHITWORTH WHITLEY Mk 5 EB287 (see fig 131)
Home Farm, Yeldersley

SK 20393 44599 (165 m) Impact site
Unit and Station: No. 42 Operational Training Unit, RAF Ashbourne, No. 38 Group
Date: 30 December 1943
Crew: four, one killed, three injured
Sergeant Edmund Anthony Farthing, pilot, killed
Three crew, unidentified, injured

When Sergeant Edmund Farthing's undercarriage would not lock down, he was advised to land on the grass to the right of the runway. Only Flying Control, realising that he was approaching to the *left* of the runway and in line with a row of houses, ordered an immediate overshoot. Sergeant Farthing was seen to power up. But moments later his Whitley stalled, crashed just short of the airfield, and exploded in flames, killing him and injuring his three crew.

The court of inquiry, finding that the pilot had lost control, suggested that in taking up their authorised crash-positions the crew had made the aircraft tail heavy. The Air Officer Commanding (the AOC) accepted this, but noted the sudden – if necessary – overshoot ordered by Flying Control. The AOC-in-Chief (his superior), however, ruled that as *Pilot's Notes* specifically warned of the Whitley's marked tendency to rear up on an overshoot, the pilot should have been ready to counter it.

Mrs Betty Hardie (née Stephens) was just five in 1943. 'This loud explosion,' she said, 'made us rush to the sitting-room window. There were these great flames, and thick black smoke. But mother didn't let me look for long. It would have been too distressing.'

How much more so, though, had the tower not ordered the overshoot!

Visiting the Site
The former airfield's environs can be variously accessed, only there is no surface evidence of the crash.

24
Ashbourne (South)

88 BRISTOL BLENHEIM Mk 4 N3567 (see fig 132)
Leys Farm, Ashbourne

SK 18269 45468 (175 m)
Unit and Station: No. 42 Operational Training Unit (OTU), RAF Ashbourne, No. 70 Group,
    Army Co-operation Command
Date: 7 November 1942
Crew: two, passenger killed, pilot injured

Flying Officer Walter Robert Mummery (Second Lieutenant, Royal Artillery, temporary RAF
   commission), pilot, injured
Aircraftman First Class Thomas Ezra Clarke, air experience, killed

Former soldier Flying Officer Walter Mummery had logged over 400 hours, including 160 hours
on the Blenheim, sixteen of which had been at night, when he was detailed for a local night-
training sortie, taking Aircraftman First Class Thomas Clarke along for the ride. Shortly after the
Blenheim lifted off, however, watchers in the tower saw its navigational lights check, then curve
downwards out of sight before a blinding flash, followed by flames, revealed black smoke rising
beyond a fringe of trees.

Crash crews quickly reached Leys Farm, some half a mile beyond the runway, where they found
Flying Officer Mummery wandering dazedly. Aircraftman Clarke, however, had been killed.

In the subsequent investigation, the focus fell upon the adjustable gills at the rear of the engine
nacelles. These were flaps that could be opened and closed to control the amount of cooling air
and so maintain the correct cylinder-head temperatures. In this case, they were found to have been
left open, although whether this had caused an unlooked-for amount of drag during the critical
stage of take off, or whether an actual loss of power had occurred, was never determined.

The court of inquiry submitted that the open cowling gills had caused the aircraft to stall. The
OTU's officer commanding, conversely, believed the gills to be immaterial, and that the pilot had
simply held too low, and had therefore struck some trees that the contractors should have felled.
Balancing both, the Air Officer Commanding ruled that the fundamental cause had been an
error of judgement by the pilot. But he also used his authority to force through the civil issue of
having the obstructive trees felled.

Mr Frank White, of Leys Farm, was seventeen at the time. 'It was about half-past eleven,' he
remembered, 'and there was a clattering like a load of milking churns. I ran to the window, and
saw that a plane had hit the trees where the houses are now. It had just scraped over Preston's
Garage, but only because, when they were building the aerodrome, they'd made John Preston
take the pitched roofs off both garage and house. They'd wanted to cut down the trees, only the
landowner wouldn't let them. But after this he had no choice.' Mr White indicated a pair of oaks
some two hundred yards from his farmhouse. 'It ended up just there, burning itself out. There'd
been a chicken coop where it landed – but there was no sign of it afterwards ...'

Flying Officer Mummery was hospitalised for some time but survived the war, relinquishing
his army commission on 5 February 1946.

Visiting the Site
The site, at Spitalhill in southern Ashbourne, is on private ground and has been periodically
chain-harrowed over the years; nevertheless, lifting a turf revealed the tell-tale blue corrosion
indicative of an aircraft crash.

89 BRISTOL BLENHEIM Mk 4 V5752 (SEE FIGS 133–134)
Blake House Farm, Ashbourne

SK 18906 44270 (159 m) Approximate site
Unit and Station: No. 42 Operational Training Unit, RAF Ashbourne, No. 70 Group, Army
   Co-operation Command
Date: 15 January 1943

Crew: three, all killed:
Pilot Officer James Norman Roberts, pilot
Two crew members, presently unidentified

Twenty minutes into a training detail, Blenheim V5752 crashed and burnt, killing all three occupants. The court of inquiry submitted that the pilot had entered cloud, and called upon to fly on instruments, had failed to maintain control, stalled, and dived into the ground.

It could be, however, that the court missed vital witness evidence. Mr Graham Parker, of Osmaston, was twelve years old at the time. 'We were used to seeing Blenheims,' he recalled, 'but what caught our attention in this case was the smoke trailing from one of its engines. Then it crashed. We ran to see it but the RAF wouldn't let us get near.'

It is commonplace for a witness to claim that a crashed aircraft was on fire before impact, but it is just possible that the pilot's loss of control in this instance was not due to his inability to fly on instruments as such, but to the additional need to deal with a troublesome engine.

Visiting the Site
The impact point, on private land, can be accessed from the Osmaston footpath. But there is nothing to see.

90 AIRSPEED OXFORD
RAF Darley Moor, Ashbourne

SK 16453 41654 (176 m)
Date: January 1943

Mr Jeff Chadfield, of Grange Farm, indicated where a twin-engined trainer had come down after suffering a power failure on take-off. 'It turned this way from Darley Moor's cross runway, hit the tree, and just sat there, slumped over.'

A visiting Oxford is known to have crashed in January 1943.

Visiting the Site
The tree still stands, but there is no trace otherwise.

25

Sudbury

91 GLOSTER METEORS F Mk 12 WS621, WS683 (SEE FIGS 135–136)
West Broughton Hollow and Sudbury Park Farm

Associated sites
SK 16460 33700 (93 m) attacking aircraft WS683 Sudbury Park Farm
SK 14602 33080 (89 m) target aircraft WS621 West Broughton Hollow
SK 19320 38400 (115 m) WS683 pilot, survivor, in tree, Alkmonton Bottoms
SK 20200 39205 (100 m) WS683 navigator's parachute, Park Style Farm
SK 14997 33071 (61 m) WS621 pilot's body, Dell Hole
SK 19010 35160 (90 m) debris, Old Myers Farm, but also widely over Sudbury Prison and Park

Unit and Station: No. 81 Group, Fighter Command, All Weather Operational Conversion Unit, RAF North Luffenham, south-east of Oakham, Rutland.
Date: 21 September 1955
Crews: four, parachuted, one killed, three survived
Pilot Officer Michael Aubrey Leslie Longman, killed, pilot WS621
Navigator of WS621, presently unidentified, landed Sudbury Park Farm
Pilot Officer Tony J. Gladwell, pilot WS683, landed Alkmonton
Navigator of WS683, presently unidentified, landed Alkmonton

While night-exercising at 20,000 feet in Meteor WS683, Pilot Officer Tony Gladwell made a diving turn to intercept WS621. At a range of just 330 yards, however, his navigator's airborne-interception radar stopped working. Pilot Officer Gladwell attempted to push beneath WS621 but after his canopy struck its belly, he and his navigator baled out at Alkmonton, their aircraft crashing and burning at Sudbury Park Farm, three miles to the south.

The crew of the target Meteor, WS621, caught totally unawares, baled out late. The navigator did so successfully. The pilot, however, Pilot Officer Longman, had his parachute snag on the tailplane before tearing free to deposit him 400 yards beyond his aircraft, which crashed and burnt out at West Broughton Hollow.

The inquiry found the untimely faulty radar to have been the main cause but recommended that initial exercises should have the attacker below the target, so making speed control easier.

The Jeffrey sisters, of Home Farm, West Broughton, heard WS621 crash. 'I thought it was thunder,' Mary recalls, 'then saw that our cabbage field was an inferno.' Her sister, Kate, remembered, 'Several lorry drivers had stopped this side of the field on what was then the main Uttoxeter Road. They could see parachute material wrapped around the tail, but the fire was too fierce for anyone to get near. And it had sliced through power cables, so they were a hazard too.'

Certainly, it was some time before the body of Pilot Officer Longman was found, in a tree, in nearby Dell Hole, now just across the A50 Trunk Road.

But as fire appliances began to arrive at West Broughton Hollow, reports were received of another jet skimming HM Prison, Sudbury, and exploding in a field at Sudbury Park Farm. Farm Manager Mr Wilf Carr was returning from a fruitless search for this aircraft when he encountered Pilot Officer Longman's navigator, who greeted him with a heartfelt, 'I could do with a pint!'

Farmer Fred Lemon and his family at Alkmonton House Farm had been alarmed by shouting and whistle blasts. The navigator of WS683, Mr Lemon found, had parachuted into a field at nearby Park Style Farm then found his pilot firmly snagged in an oak at Alkmonton Bottoms. Using a ladder, Mr Lemon managed to release Pilot Officer Gladwell, then took both airmen to his wife, Joan, for much-welcomed cups of tea.

'Pieces of aircraft,' remembered Mrs Barbara Grave, who lived in Sudbury Prison married quarters, 'littered the ground in both the Prison and the Park.'

Visiting the Site
Tracing this train of events provides a good spread of flat walks, but with nothing to be seen of the incident at any of the sites.

92 DE HAVILLAND DH82A TIGER MOTH (SEE FIGS 137–138)
Muselane Farm, Aston Heath

SK 17538 33039 (78 m)
Unit and Station: No. 16 Elementary Flying Training School, RAF Burnaston, Derby, No. 51
    Group, Flying Training Command
Date: 1943
Crew: two, unidentified, but unhurt

Mr Harold Nash, of Muselane Farm, Aston Heath, near Sudbury, and his three sisters, the Misses Amy, Bessie, and Dorothy, readily remembered this Tiger Moth incident.

'It tried to make a landing in the field opposite the house,' Mr Nash recalled, 'but it crashed into a wooden fence at the far end, although nobody was hurt.'

'Airmen were sent from Burnaston,' Sister Bessie remembered. 'We put them up in the hayloft. And next day they took the plane away on a low loader.'

Very likely a forced-landing exercise during which the sparking plugs had been allowed to oil up while idling on the approach. But left without power, it then became a problem of stopping the brakeless Tiger Moth. Almost certainly, however, this would have been treated as just one of the hazards attendant upon elementary flying training.

Visiting the Site
It is unlikely that anything was left by the salvage crew. Certainly, there is nothing to see now.

26
Belper

93 NORTH AMERICAN HARVARD KF570 (SEE FIG 139)
Postern Hill Farm, Hazelwood

SK 32480 46372 (153 m) touchdown
SK 32151 46180 (132 m) terminal site
Unit and Station: No. 6 Service Flying Training School, RAF Ternhill, near Market Drayton,
  Shropshire, No. 23 Group, Flying Training Command
Date: 16 January 1947
Crew: two, both injured
Flight Sergeant George King
Flight Sergeant Robert William Baird

On 16 January 1947 Sergeant Pilot George King, accompanied by Sergeant Robert William Baird, got airborne from RAF Ternhill to carry out an envisaged thirty-minute air test. It was the year of the big snow, however, and he got lost and, unable to establish radio contact, eventually decided to put down before true darkness fell and the fuel ran out. Chancing to overfly the lights of a hamlet, he then found himself skimming a pasture near a farmhouse, and hastily closed the throttle. He had not realised, however, how sharply the ground fell away, consequently the need to drop the nose more than expected, allied to the unfamiliar attitude required to settle to the ground without his undercarriage, caused him to strike hard. The aircraft bellied on, clipping a tree then burying itself in a hedge, sustaining severe damage to the wings and propeller. The occupants, though shocked, were not seriously hurt.

A little later, Mrs Elizabeth Spendlove, of Postern Hill Farm, was surprised to find herself confronted by two shaken and bloodstained airmen. Just the same, only after bandaging their cuts and serving them with cups of tea did she turn to the task of alerting the authorities.

The court of inquiry submitted that Sergeant George should have carried out a precautionary landing before darkness overtook him, alternatively, that he and his passenger should have baled out. His flying log book was duly endorsed – a wrist slap.

Mr Arthur Chadderton, then working at Postern Lodge Farm, was able to point out the crash site. 'We saw it next day,' he said, 'indeed, it stayed there for some time.'

Visiting the Site
No public footpath runs near the site, and no trace remains.

Miles Magister, Bonsall
See page 127

118. The set-down site of a Magister, with Upper Town to the left.

De Havilland Tiger Moth BB811, Dethick
See page 128

119. The site of the misjudged precautionary landing of Tiger Moth BB811.

Miles Magister L8277, Colliery Farm
See page 128

Left: **120.** From the impact area of Magister L8277 along 10-Acre Field, with Colliery Farm to the left.

Avro Anson Mk 2, Mount Pleasant Farm
See page 129

Below: **121.** Looking back along the approach of the Anson which landed at Mount Pleasant Farm.

Armstrong Whitworth Albemarle V1604,
Bradley Pastures
See page 130

Top: **122.** The impact area of Albemarle V1604.

Left: **123.** Mr Ray Archer, with debris from V1604.

Albemarle P1463, Wigber Low
See page 131

Above: **124.** The impact site of Albemarle P1463.

Europa G-KWIP, Bradley
See page 132

Right: **125.** Mr Tom Lawton at the impact point of Europa G-KWIP.

126. (Inset) The crashed Europa.

Armstrong Whitworth Whitley, Holly Meadow
See page 133

Left: **127.** Mr Tom Lawton at the terminal site of the Whitley at Holly Meadow Farm.

Armstrong Whitworth Whitley, Hole in the Wall
See page 133

Below: **128.** The impact point of the Whitley at Hole in the Wall, with the terminal site in the field beyond.

Miles Magister T9823, Hallfield
See page 134

129. The impact site of Magister T9823, with importunate incumbents.

Armstrong Whitworth Whitley EB337, Crowtrees Farm
See page 135

130. The set-down site of Whitley EB337, beside the A517.

Armstrong Whitworth Whitley EB287, Home Farm

See page 135

131. Betty Stephens (later Mrs Betty Hardie), on right, with her brother and adult family friend. The Whitley is Z6628.

Bristol Blenheim Mk 4 N3567, Leys Farm
See page 136

132. The terminal site of Blenheim N3567, with corroded debris, looking back down the line of flight.

Bristol Blenheim Mk 4 V5752, Blake House
See page 137

Above: **133.** The impact site, looking towards Blake House.

Right: **134.** Mr Graham Parker, witness.

Gloster Meteors F Mk 12 WS621 and WS683, West Broughton
See page 138

135. Impact site of Meteor WS621, Sudbury Park Farm.

136. Mr Barry Carr, his back to the impact site of WS683, Sudbury Park Farm.

De Havilland Tiger Moth, Muselane Farm
See page 139

137. De Havilland Tiger Moth.

138. Looking from the fence line, back along the approach of the Tiger Moth which landed at Muselane Farm.

94 VICKERS WELLINGTON Mk 1C DV435 (see fig 140)
Shottle Hall, Belper

SK 30731 47840 (131 m)

Unit and Station: No. 14 Operational Training Unit (OTU), RAF Market Harborough, No. 92
    (Training) Group, Bomber Command

Date: 24 November 1943

Crew: four, parachuted, one killed

Flying Officer D. W. A. Stewart, pilot

Flying Officer Joseph Norman Clark, navigator/air bomber, RNZAF, injured

Sergeant J. Ould, wireless operator, injured

Sergeant John Donald Hall, air gunner, killed

On returning from a training flight, Flying Officer Stewart encountered such severe icing that he found himself unable to maintain control. He ordered his crew to abandon, but the rear gunner, Sergeant John Hall, was killed. The Wellington crashed into a field at Shottle Hall and burst into flames, but caused no collateral damage other than a crater.

The RAF investigators were unable to determine the reason for Sergeant Hall's death, but as they especially noted 'pilot acted OK', it suggests that they were satisfied that Flying Officer Stewart had seen his crew away in good time.

The survivors completed their courses, but New Zealander Flying Officer Joseph Clark was killed on 16 November 1944 during Lancaster operations from RAF Spilsby.

Mr and Mrs Herbert and Myrtle Slater, formerly of Overlane, recalled the crash. 'We heard this crash,' said Mrs Slater, 'and saw this great yellow flame.'

'From White Lane,' Herbert added, 'we could see that the plane had come down at the back of the hay barn. There was wreckage everywhere, still burning, and it was said that two of the crew had been discovered wandering near Round Wood.'

'For years,' said Mr Jeff Butler of Shottle Hall Cottages, 'you'd plough up bits of aluminium, but in a very localised area. Since then, though, a Derby historical group did a dig.'

Visiting the Site
The site, south of Shottle, is just yards from a public footpath, accessed from Lambhouse Lane or White Lane. No surface debris was found.

27

Derby

95 MILES MASTER Mk 1 T8685 (see figs 141–142)
Denby Common, west of Heanor

SK 40800 47150 (107 m) touchdown

SK 40902 47226 (138 m) terminal site

Unit and Station: No. 5 Service Flying Training School, RAF Ternhill, Market Drayton, No. 21
    Group, Flying Training Command
Date: 25 September 1941
Crew: pilot, injured
Leading Aircraftman G. B. Garland, injured

Pupil pilot Leading Aircraftman G. B. Garland had just under one hundred hours flying time
when, having been sent on a solo sortie from RAF Ternhill to practise spins, steep turns, and
forced-landings, he got lost and had to set-down in earnest. The field he selected, however, on the
edge of Denby Common and some forty-six miles from his Shropshire base, was not only planted
with anti-invasion stakes but rose steeply. The slope forced him to ease up the nose to avoid too
heavy a touch down. Only this delayed him making ground contact. Running out of space, he
applied full power to overshoot but struck a pole, losing one of his wings then breasting through
a hedge to bring up in the yard of a pair of cottages. The Master burst into flames but Leading
Aircraftman Garland was able to scramble clear.

    The court of inquiry deemed the field chosen to be quite unsuitable, and further ruled that, though
lost, Leading Aircraftman Garland had failed to make a 'reasoned and systematic attempt to establish
his position'. Even so, the incident was regarded as a natural hazard attendant upon flying training.

    Mrs Mavis March (née Orme), still living in the neighbouring, non-involved cottage, recalled,
'Had Mrs Bardell – Elizabeth – been in her kitchen she wouldn't have survived, for the plane's
nose was up against her kitchen door and the flames burnt through it and the kitchen window
and up the back wall to the bedroom where she was.'

Visiting the Site
The site is just off the Denby-Loscoe Road, the house remaining, of course, a private residence.
However, a footpath running through the set-down field provides a good viewpoint.

96 AIRSPEED OXFORD N4597 (see fig 143)
Elm Farm, Little Eaton, Derbyshire

SK 36007 41364 (54 m)
Unit and Station: No. 21 (Pilots) Advanced Flying Unit, RAF Seighford, north-west of
    Stafford, No. 21 Group, Flying Training Command
Date: 13 July 1945
Crew: pilot, killed
Flight Sergeant Lancelot Percy Williamson

Having been authorised for a local-area staff-continuation sortie, Flight Sergeant Lancelot
Williamson made his way instead to Little Eaton where, positioning from the Derby direction,
he carried out a sustained dive to pass low over a row of thatched cottages [since demolished].
He failed to check his dive sufficiently, however, brushed the upper branches of a tree, and was
killed on crashing in the fields immediately beyond.

    'My mother,' Mr John Easter, of Little Eaton recounted, 'saw this aircraft pass very low and very
fast overhead. It then went behind Elm Farm and hit one of the trees in The Lawns, the debris – and
the pilot's body – spilling over into Brickyard Field. Of course, us local lads rushed to the scene but
the RAF soon sealed it off. The pilot was initially taken to a room in the railway station.'

The court of inquiry found that, 'While carrying out unauthorised low flying pilot allowed aircraft to hit a tree, causing the aircraft to disintegrate'. Technically, they observed that he had either misjudged his height or too tardily pulled out of his dive. But each reporting officer in turn agreed that the accident had been a 'flagrant disobedience of orders', the most senior directing that 'full publicity should be given this accident throughout the RAF'. Clearly, with the war manifestly in its last stages, the Service was anxious to ensure that no slackness in flying standards was to be allowed to creep in.

Visiting the Site
Only the obstructing tree gave evidence in 2012.

97 DE HAVILLAND DH82A TIGER MOTH
Morley Lane, east of Little Eaton

SK 37371 41774 (134 m)
Unit and Station: Not known, Flying Training Command
Date: early 1942
Crew: not recorded

Mr John Easter, of Little Eaton, recalled, 'Towards Morley Lane this Tiger Moth was upended over a hedge but didn't seem that badly damaged.'

No further details have come to light. But Mr Easter continued, 'Some weeks later I saw the Wellington on pressurisation-trials lose a wing over Stanley.' [Wellington W5795, which crashed on 12 July 1942 but is outside the geographical scope of this series]

28
West of Derby

98 MILES MAGISTER Mᴋ 1 L8227 (ꜱᴇᴇ ꜰɪɢ 144)
Long Lane, Lees, near Derby

SK 26711 38036 (98 m)
Unit and Station: No. 16 Elementary Flying Training School, RAF Burnaston, Derby, No. 51
    Group, Flying Training Command
Date: 21 June 1942
Crew: two, instructor, killed; pupil, injured
Pilot Officer Godfrey Harry Grantham, RAF Volunteer Reserve, killed
Corporal J. P. Ward, army, pupil pilot, injured

On returning from a navigational sortie, instructor Pilot Officer Grantham initiated a forced-landing drill, closing the throttle and leaving his soldier pupil, Corporal Ward, to select a landing site and carry out an approach. Corporal Ward chose a very adequate pasture to the north of

Long Lane, at Lees, but in the course of a gliding turn stalled the aircraft into the ground from an estimated 200 feet. Pilot Officer Grantham was killed, and Corporal Ward injured.

The court of inquiry found the primary cause to be an error of judgement by the instructor in not assuming control before the situation became critical.

Mr Lawrence Alcock, of Fold Farm, Lees, identified the crash site, remembering. 'I was biking west down Long Lane when I saw this Maggie in the hedge. Our former local fire chief had already got the pilot's body from the cockpit and was laying it out.'

Visiting the Site
A footpath leaving Long Lane opposite Cherry Tree Farm passes the site but there is no visible evidence.

99 MILES MAGISTER Mk 1 N3876 (see fig 145)
Culland Hall, Hollington

SK 24516 39062 (102 m)
Unit and Station: No. 30 Elementary Flying Training School, RAF Burnaston, Derby, No. 51
    Group, Flying Training Command
Date: 21 September 1939

This aircraft crashed on hitting a tree during aerobatics. The crash-report summary offers nothing else and no further details are known.

Visiting the Site
The area is well served by footpaths, one of which passes the site.

100 MILES MAGISTER Mk 1 N3813 (see fig 146)
Roston, near Rocester

SK 14141 40577 (161 m)
Unit and Station: No. 16 Elementary Flying Training School, RAF Burnaston, Derby, No. 51
    Group, Flying Training Command
Date: 18 August 1940
Crew: pilot, badly injured
Flying Officer R. Hope

While carrying out aerobatics and forced-landing approaches, Flying Officer Hope realised that he was short of fuel. In setting down, however, he stalled and crashed, sustaining severe injuries.

The court of inquiry duly found that the stall had caused the crash but also that Flying Officer Hope had departed with insufficient fuel. His instructor, a Sergeant Greenup, was disciplined.

Mr Alan Wood and his wife, Viola, of Bank End Farm, Roston, were able to indicate the crash site. 'My nephews,' Mrs Wood remembered, 'brought away a compass. But dad made them take it back. Only when they came up out of the Dumble again, guards had been posted.'

Visiting the Site

There is no trace of the crash. But the 'Dumble' remains a vegetation-choked gully separating Roston from the fields where the aircraft crashed – now combined as Ten Acre Field. The most direct access, having branched off a public footpath leaving the Roston–Roston Common Road at SK 14256 40857, requires negotiation of the deepest of field ditches. Indeed, local farmer Mr Jeff Chadfield remembered a bullock, missing for 24 hours, found trapped and barely visible in its depths.

29

Church Broughton

101 VICKERS WELLINGTON Mk 3 BK405 (see figs 147–149)
Covert Farm, Boylestone

SK 20373 353578 (94 m)
Unit and Station: No. 27 Operational Training Unit, RAF Church Broughton, No. 93 Group,
    Bomber Command
Date: 11 January 1943
Crew: five, all killed
Flying Officer Ralph Holland Tye, Royal New Zealand Air Force, staff pilot
Sergeant William Raymond Wearne, Royal Australian Air Force, pupil pilot
Sergeant Ian Ross McDonald, RAAF, navigator
Sergeant J. Kerr, RAFVR, wireless operator/air gunner
Sergeant John Stoppard Eccles, RAAF, air gunner

Five minutes into a training sortie that was to include single-engined operation, Wellington BK405 entered a spin and crashed, bursting into flames and killing all on board.

Although the investigators were forced to speculate, they concluded that Warrant Officer Tye, positioned by Sergeant Wearne's shoulder, had cut the left-hand engine to simulate its having failed. Subsequently, however, the 'cut-off' control for the right-hand engine had been operated. After that, because BK405 lacked dual controls, the instructor had been unable to retrieve the situation.

It is noteworthy that the unit's commanding officer felt that the accident had been caused because the 'pupil turned into the dead engine', so reflecting the fallacious belief of the era that to turn towards a stopped engine was fatal.

Mr John Wall, of Sudbury, had run to the crash from school. 'When we got there,' he recalled, 'they were trying to extract the bodies with long rakes. No-one noticed us, but the sight took a long time to get out of our minds.'

Mr William Smith, owner of Covert Farm, confirmed the location.

Visiting the Site

The site is on private land, but authorised access would be from a farm track-cum-footpath leaving Ashbourne Road opposite Bartonpark, just south of Covert Farm. The site, from which ploughed-up debris scraps still emerge, is marked by the single oak that remains from what was in 1943 a southwest–

northeast-aligned hedgerow. Three of the crew are buried in Scropton Churchyard Extension.

102 VICKERS WELLINGTON Mk 3 BK241 (SEE FIGS 150–151)
Osleston Hall Farm, Osleston

SK 24837 36944 (117 m)
Unit and Station: No. 27 Operational Training Unit, RAF Church Broughton, No. 93 Group,
    Bomber Command
Date: 3 February 1943
Crew: five, all killed
Sergeant Frederick George Bell, Royal Australian Air Force, pilot
Sergeant Raymond Knight Hodson, Royal Australian Air Force, supernumerary pilot
Sergeant Arthur William Reid, RAF, navigator
Sergeant Frederick James Keown, RAF, wireless operator/air gunner
Sergeant Kevin Vincent Howes, RAAF, air bomber

Sergeant Frederick Bell was circling Church Broughton, waiting to join the circuit, when his aircraft fell into a spin to the right, possibly a flat spin – in practical terms an irrecoverable condition, especially at low level. An escape hatch in the belly was jettisoned, but the aircraft hit the ground, leaving no survivors.

After much deliberation, the court of inquiry submitted that the disposition of the training ballast carried, in addition to the weight of the rear gunner, had altered the centre of gravity and caused the spin to go flat. Although higher authority would not entertain that theory, no alternative explanation was advanced.

Mr George Sessions, of Osleston Hall Farm, remembered the crash only too clearly. 'I was on the way up to bed when I saw the Wellington's lights through the window. It was turning, and so low that I thought it would run into Osleston House, over the road. But then there was a thud – nothing more – as it went into the field beyond.' He paused. 'A young Australian seemed to be just sitting against the side gate. He'd a cut below his eye. Otherwise even his parting was unruffled. We laid him alongside the others by the hedge at the field entrance.' He went on, 'The tail was in the hedge, and the engines about thirty yards into the field. But the escape hatch was further away, where they'd thrown it out. Only they'd been too late. Besides, it was said they'd been too low to jump …'

He paused. 'I had to plough this whole top-diagonal corner to bury the bits.'

Visiting the Site
The site is on private ground, although a footpath traverses the farm. The site, however, has been well been dug over by enthusiasts and there is nothing to see. Four of the crew are buried in Scropton Churchyard extension.

103 VICKERS WELLINGTON Mk 3 BJ904 (SEE FIGS 152–153)
Conygree Wood, Church Broughton

SK 19798 32730 (74 m)
Unit and Station: No. 27 Operational Training Unit, RAF Church Broughton, No. 93 Group,
    Bomber Command

Date: 19 June 1944
Crew: six, three killed, three injured
Flight Sergeant Lewis Keith Maxwell, Royal Australian Air Force, pilot, killed
Flight Sergeant Rowan Burgess Sterling, RAAF, killed
Sergeant Allan Warren Shiels, RAAF, killed
Pilot Officer W. G. Moeller, RAAF, injured
Sergeant W. D. Smout, RAAF, injured
Sergeant Schodde, RAAF, injured

As Flight Sergeant Lewis Maxwell and his all-Australian trainee crew arrived back at Church Broughton from a six-and-a-half-hour training sortie, his left engine stopped. With its propeller windmilling he was unable to maintain directional control, swung left, and crashed into Conygree Wood, the aircraft ploughing through a raft of felled tree trunks. Three crew members were killed.

The court of inquiry, finding that the left engine had cut from lack of fuel, recommended that in future, when flights exceeded three hours, aircraft should land and re-fuel before carrying out additional exercises.

Schoolboy John Wall was playing in the pasture of Marle Pit Farm when Wellington BJ904 swept overhead, though living so close to the runway, near-miss crashes were by no means unusual. Mr Morris Goodwin, a family friend, however, exclaimed, 'I'd hate to live here. It's far too risky.'

Yet just five months later, on 27 November 1944, Mr Goodwin, his wife, and his sister-in-law, having left their own farm for market, turned back on meeting a delivery van. Minutes later, they were among the seventy persons killed when part of the RAF bomb-dump in the Fauld gypsum caverns exploded, instantly transforming their hill-top farm into a reeking hollow …

Visiting the Site

Conygree Wood shows no sign of the crash. The Fauld crater, however (accessed at SK 18054 28013), still takes a good twenty minutes to walk around.

104 VICKERS WELLINGTON Mk 3 BK252 (SEE FIGS 154–155)
Cotefield Farm, Church Broughton

SK 19400 33150 (83 m)
Unit and Station: No. 27 Operational Training Unit, RAF Church Broughton, No. 93 Group,
    Bomber Command
Date: 6 September 1944
Crew: six, two killed, four injured, all Royal Australian Air Force
Flight Sergeant Alan Livingstone Currie, pilot, killed
Flight Sergeant Reginald Arthur Groves, killed
Flight Sergeant Newnham
Flight Sergeant Heal
Flight Sergeant Hennesey
Sergeant McDougall

Having overshot from an approach, Wellington BK252 was seen to swerve, then strike the ground. Bouncing high, it took the chimney off Woodhouse Farm, crossed a cornfield and impacted against the far bank of a pond. Four crew members survived.

Though the station's technicians could find no evidence of an engine failure, the manufacturers confirmed that some defect had, indeed, occurred. Higher authority, accepting this as the root cause, commented that on one engine, with full flap, and the undercarriage still down, it would have been 'virtually impossible [for the pilot] to maintain either height or control'.

Mr John Wall, then a lad, seeing the aircraft pass his window, shouted, 'Dad, there's a plane crashing!' But to this day he wonders at the escape of Mr Sam Frost, of Woodhouse Farm, who had been attending to his front gate when the aircraft leaped his cottage, bringing the chimney stack down around him.

Visiting the Site
No surface evidence remains.

105 VICKERS WELLINGTON Mk 13 NC661 (see pages 156–157)
Trusley, west of Derby

SK 25343 36010 (91 m)
Unit and Station: RAF Shawbury, No. 25 Group, Flying Training Command
Date: 25 June 1946
Occupants: six, all killed. Four crew, two Air Training Corps cadets
Crew
Warrant Officer J. H. B. Livett, pilot
Flight Lieutenant David Bowie, DFM, navigator
Flying Officer John Stanley May, RAFVR, navigator/bomb aimer
Warrant Officer Maurice Madams, RAFVR, wireless operator/air gunner
Passengers
Cadet Robert Sydney Wallace, No. 493 Squadron, Air Training Corps
Cadet Geoffrey Peter Balty, No. 493 Squadron, Air Training Corps

When Warrant Officer Livett took off on a cross-country exercise on 25 June 1946, his three-man crew was augmented by two seventeen-year-old Air Training Corps cadets enjoying an air-experience flight. Just forty minutes later, however, his aircraft was seen over Burnaston airfield, near Derby, flying at an estimated 1,000 feet with one engine stopped and its propeller feathered.

Instead of landing at Burnaston, however, Warrant Officer Livett turned towards RAF Church Broughton whose controller, recognising that the Wellington was in difficulties, signalled an immediate landing clearance. Possibly not having seen either airfield, Warrant Officer Livett turned away north-eastwards and began an approach to a wheatfield at The Elms, to the west of Trusley village. He floated too far, though, and attempted an overshoot, but clipped a tree. The aircraft then struck a beech coppice and slammed into the ground, gouging away the tops of the ridge-and-furrow undulations before nosing into a second coppice, exploding in flames, and killing all on board.

The fact that the court of inquiry criticised Warrant Officer Livett for not landing at Church Broughton suggests that some mutual communication between tower and aircraft – other than the green Very cartridge fired by the tower – had, in fact, been established. More decidedly, having further criticised him for not having more ably handled either the set-down or the overshoot, higher authority decreed that staff pilots should receive more continuation training.

Farmer Ted Durose, of Willows Farm, Trusley, then a lad of thirteen, looked up to see, 'What I took for a Wellington. But later an airman at the site told me it wasn't a Wellington, but a Warwick ...'

This initial mis-identification came about because the control towers at Burnaston and Church Broughton were more used to seeing Wellington training-variants and took the Mark 13 maritime version – with four radar masts along its back – for the Warwick, the slightly-larger stablemate of the Wellington often employed with Coastal Command.

Visiting the Site

Nearby footpaths abound although the terminal site is on private land and has long been used as a tip. As Farmer Robin Goodall noted, even those beeches which survived the conflagration became hazardous and were felled.

106 DE HAVILLAND DH82A TIGER MOTH (see fig 158)
Goldhurst Farm, Trusley

SK 25318 34483 64 m
Unit and Station: No. 16 (Polish) Service Flying Training School, RAF Newton, No. 21 Group,
    Flying Training Command
Date: 1940–41
Crew: Polish pupil pilot, unhurt

Mr Joe Tunnicliffe held that during the early war years it was so common for Tiger Moths and Magisters to put down locally that it was hardly worth facing the music for rushing from the playground to visit them. However, to have two on the ground, he conceded, was unusual enough.

'It would have been late in 1940, possibly 1941, I suppose,' he said, 'and this particular Tiger Moth came over Trusley Old Hall and put down in the field right beside Goldhurst Farm, stopping nosed up to the spinney. And as it was out of fuel, that's where it stayed overnight.'

Mr Ted Durose, of Common Piece Farm – now Willows Farm – remembered its pilot. 'He had an RAF battledress, but with "Poland" on the shoulders. He'd obviously been told at Goldhurst Farm that we'd got a phone. But when he finally got through all we could understand was that he was, "Seven miles souse-souse-west of Derby." Only "souse" was what we called the meat from pigs' faces. Anyhow, next morning another Tiger Moth landed with two pilots and cans of fuel. And having refuelled the first one, they both took off.' He smiled. 'The first one, the pupil, I suppose, climbed away normally enough. But the second only just cleared the far end of the big field before he started to climb.'

Clearly the instructor, temporarily freed from his mentoring cares, had held the Tiger Moth down until the last possible moment before letting it zoom skywards.

Not a crash, as such. But for the interested walker an incident which encapsulates so much of the flavour of those far-gone days, when not everything under the sun was dire.

30

Radbourne

107 VICKERS WELLINGTON Mk 3 BK508
Terrel Hays, Radbourne

SK 27802 35066 (88 m)

Unit and Station: No. 27 Operational Training Unit, RAF Church Broughton, No. 93 Group,
   Bomber Command

Date: 4 April 1943

Crew: five, one killed, four survived, injured

Sergeant Law, pilot

Sergeant Peter Adolphus White, RAF, air bomber, killed

Three other crew members, presently unidentified, injured

Sergeant Law was carrying out a general-handling detail whose secondary aim was to air-test the machine in preparation for night-flying training. An hour into the flight, however, after some circuits and overshoots, his right-hand engine began to run roughly. He nursed it along until he was in a position to turn onto the crosswind – the penultimate – leg of his circuit. But even as he did so, it stopped abruptly.

Mr Norman Wall was up a ladder at Sutton on the Hill. 'The plane,' he said, 'seemed to be just staggering through the air, and descending too.'

Mr John Litchfield, then of Hall Farm, Dalbury, seeing that the Wellington's wheels were down, called out to his helper, 'Walter! It's coming in to land.'

The court of inquiry would say that Sergeant Law should have had no real problem. He still had 900 feet in hand, the weather was good, and from the crosswind leg it was all downhill. As it was, retracting his undercarriage, he decided to land immediately.

Mr Litchfield was a reluctant witness. 'He had the very worst of luck,' he said, 'for after some low power wires and a tree-studded hedge, it was all open pasture. He missed the wires all right. But hit and shattered the centre tree. This brought his nose down, and his tail up, the impact showering the field with debris.'

He paused. 'When we got there the tail was upright with the fuselage blazing furiously from deep ditch.' He paused again. 'I saw this hand, held out to me … Then it disappeared. Only at that moment the heat got to me, and I ran back behind the hedge to where it was, at least, bearable …' He shook his head. 'I've tried ever since to persuade myself that I did everything I possibly could have!'

That his feeling of inadequacy was misplaced was shown by an experienced fireman who mouthed to him, 'Isn't it a bugger? For you haven't a hope of achieving anything.'

The court of inquiry discovered that an engine component had failed. Still it submitted that the pilot should have been capable of safely getting down on the airfield. The Air Officer Commanding allowed further that the three overshoots carried out had probably imposed 'great strains on the engine'. A lofty observation which undoubtedly raised some eyebrows.

Visiting the Site

The site is by the crossroads at Terrel Hays. Pylons erected in 1954 replace the lower, wooden poles avoided by the Wellington and although one of the trees remain, it would be unusual to find surface evidence.

108 DE HAVILLAND HORNET F1 PX244 (SEE FIGS 158–159)
Foxfields Farm, Radbourne, 6 miles north-west of Derby

SK 27358 36348 (87 m) hedge
SK 27300 36400 (90 m) terminal site
Unit and Station: No. 41 Squadron, RAF Church Fenton, south-west of York, No. 12 Group,
    Fighter Command
Date: 4 November 1948
Crew: pilot, unhurt
P2 [Sergeant] Emrys Victor George

When P2 Emrys George suffered a double engine failure at 8,000 feet, he made a forced-landing at Foxfields Farm but struck a hedge, ripping off the right wing and slewing the aircraft around.

The court of inquiry observed that inadvertently switching off both ignition switches would have caused both engines to fail, although whether they were graceless enough to put this to the pilot is not known … Having considered icing and a refuelling discrepancy, however, they proffered that the cause had been an obscure and unexplained technical failure, with no blame attaching to anyone. The Air Officer Commanding, though, had the court re-opened to search for further evidence but when none was forthcoming accepted a finding of 'an unexplained technical failure', the AOC-in-Chief concurring.

Local farmer Mr Gordon Johnson was able to mark on the map where debris scraps were subsequently detected.

Visiting the Site

The site is most easily accessed from the Bonnie Prince Charlie Walk, on Heage Lane, just south-west of Radbourne. In 1954 power lines were erected and only a few trees remain of the former hedge – still shown on some maps. The Hornet's landing run terminated just short of Radbourne Brook, but no surface evidence remains.

31
South of A50 (Scropton)

109 VICKERS WELLINGTON T.10 JA343 (SEE FIG 160)
Lemon's Holme, Scropton

SK 19200 31290 (60 m) (RAF report: 1 mile south-south-west of Church Broughton)
Unit and Station: RAF Church Broughton, No. 27 Operational Training Unit, No. 93 Group,
    Bomber Command
Date: 8 November 1944
Crew: six, all killed:
Sergeant John Spurgeon Hood, Royal Canadian Air Force, pilot
Sergeant Harold Lawson Fernstrom, RCAF, navigator
Sergeant James Frederick Gazzard, RCAF, air bomber
Sergeant Bernard Ivor Williams, RAFVR, wireless operator/air gunner
Sergeant William J. Drozdiak, RCAF, air gunner
Sergeant Athol White, Royal Australian Air Force, air gunner

Wellington JA343, a Mark 10, the dedicated trainer version of the type, got airborne from
RAF Church Broughton on a night training exercise under the command of Sergeant John
Hood, RCAF. Twenty minutes into the sortie, however, he lost control in cloud, the aircraft
disintegrating and crashing in flames, killing all on board.

Technical examination determined that an excessive download imposed during an uncontrolled
dive had caused the wings to fracture, the rudder, fin, and elevator parting subsequently.

Mr Terry Woodhall, a lad of six in 1944, remembered, 'One wing fell across the stream running
down the Watery Lane Wood, so we used it as a bridge.'

Pressed to positively differentiate between this November 1944 crash and the October 1942
crash site of Wellington Z8854 (below), just yards distant on the far side of Watery Lane – a
recurrent problem in locating sites near this busy training airfield – Mr Woodhall reasoned that
in 1942 he would only have been four, and not allowed to roam.

Visiting the Site
The impact site of the detached wing is the only one determined, all others having been eradicated
during construction of the A50 and the re-direction of local roads, not least Watery Lane itself.

North American Harvard KF570, Hazelwood
See page 140

139. The terminal crash site of Harvard KF570.

Vickers Wellington Mk 1C DV435, Shottle Hall
See page 141

140. The impact site of Wellington DV435, looking towards Shottle Hall.

Miles Master Mk 1 T8685, Denby Common
See page 152

141. Mrs Mavis March, showing where Master T8685 struck.

142. (Inset) The initial impact point; the cottage struck is to the right.

Airspeed Oxford N4597, Elm Farm
See page 152

143. The tree Flight Sergeant Williamson clipped in Oxford N4597.

Miles Magister L8227,
Long Lane
See page 154

144. The impact site of
Magister L8227.

Miles Magister N3876,
Culland Hall
See page 154

145. The impact site of
Magister N3876.

Miles Magister N3813,
Royston
See page 155

146. The impact site
of Magister N3813,
Roston.

Vickers Wellington Mk 3 BK405, Covert Farm
See page 155

147. Professor Sean Moran at the impact area of BK405; the vehicle is at the field entrance.

148. A memento of Wellington BK405, held at Covert Farm.:

149. Ploughed-up surface debris, 2012.

Vickers Wellington Mk 3 BK241, Osleston Farm
See page 156

150. Looking towards the field gate from the terminal impact site of Wellington BK241. This whole area was covered in debris.

151. Debris evidence from BK241 in early 2012.

Vickers Wellington Mk 3 BJ904, Conygree Wood
See page 157

152. Mr John Wall at the crash site of Wellington BJ904. The trees have grown since the crash.

Inset: **153.** The Fauld Crater.

Vikcers Wellington Mk 3
BK252, Cotefield Farm
See page 158

154. The restored chimney struck by Wellington BK252.

Above left: **155.** Mr John Wall at the terminal crash site of Wellington BK252.

Vickers Wellington Mk 13 NC661, Trusley
See page 158

Above right: **156.** Mr Robin Goodall, of Ivy Close Farm. A beech copse before the crash of Wellington NC661, the impact crater has long been a tip.

157. The crash scene. (Courtesy of the *Derby Evening Telegraph*)

De Havilland Hornet F 1 PX244,
Foxfields Farm
See page 161

Top: **158.** At the termination site.

Middle: **159.** Hornet PX244 in the hands of the salvage crew, looking towards Radbourne Brook.

Vickers Wellington T.10 JA343, Lemon's Holme
See page 162

Bottom: **160.** The ditch beside Watery Lane Wood, bridged by a wing section from Wellington JA343.

Vickers Wellington T.10 HZ533, Brookhouse Farm
See page 163

161. The impact site of Wellington HZ533, looking across Scropton and towards Church Broughton.

Percival Prentice VS645, Foston Hall Woods
See page 172

162. The impact site of Prentice VS645. Foston Hall is screened by the woods beyond the recently erected fence.

163. (Inset) Cadet Pilot Barbara Gubbins, WRAF Reserve.

110 VICKERS WELLINGTON Mᴋ 1 Z8854
Watery Lane, Scropton

SK 19546 31491 (58 m)
Unit and Station: No. 27 Operational Training Unit, RAF Church Broughton, No. 93 Group,
  Bomber Command
Date: 13 October 1942
Crew: six, Czechoslovakians, inducted into the Royal Air Force Voluntary Reserve (*Let. V Zál*),
  all killed
Flight Lieutenant Frantisec Fanta, OTU staff pilot (*Npor: Nadporučík*)
Flight Sergeant Josef Hrala, pilot (*Rt:* Rotmistr)
Warrant Officer Miroslaw Mucha, navigator (*Ppor: Praporčík*)
Flying Officer Václav Obšil, wireless operator (*Ppor*)
Sergeant Emil Tŭrkl, air gunner (*Svob: Svobodník, [substantive Czech rank, Leading Aircraftman]*)
Flight Sergeant Rudolf Jelínek, air gunner (*Rt*)

On their return from a dual, night cross-country flight, the Czechoslovakian trainee crew found
that the Church Broughton weather had turned foggy. That being the case, staff pilot Flight
Lieutenant Frantisec Fanta would have been closely monitoring the pupil pilot, Flight Sergeant
Josef Hrala, as he set up a circuit preparatory to flying the steep, circling, final-approach path
called for when landing visually in such conditions. Only the aircraft flew into the ground half a
mile short of the runway, exploding in flames, and killing all on board.

Pondering the loss of control, the unit commander went on record with 'Cannot understand
why!' But the investigators were equally mystified. And as neither the Air Officer Commanding
nor the AOC-in-Chief had anything to offer, the incident was closed.

Just the same, a reasonable speculation would be that on the last stage of the finals turn Flight
Sergeant Hrala lost the lights and became disorientated. Then, lacking visual cues, and not having
maintained an adequate instrument scan, he did not realise that the turn was steepening and the
descent rate increasing even more than planned, so taking his aircraft into the ground.

Visiting the Site
An early visitor, Mr John Wall, of Sudbury Park, remembered that the salvage team left the
ground littered with fragments. The site itself, though, was subsequently obliterated during the
construction of the A57 trunk road. The crew are buried in Scropton Churchyard Extension.

111 VICKERS WELLINGTON T.10 HZ533 (ꜱᴇᴇ ꜰɪɢ 161)
Brookhouse Farm

SK 18316 29974 (58m)
Unit and Station: No. 27 Operational Training Unit, RAF Church Broughton, No. 93 Group,
  Bomber Command
Date: 18 December 1944
Crew: five, four killed, one injured
Flight Sergeant Donald Danford Westphal, pilot, Royal Australian Air Force
Flight Sergeant John Murray Irvine, RAAF, navigator
Flight Sergeant George Thomas Miller, RAAF, air bomber

Flight Sergeant Angus Murdock McPhail, RAAF, wireless operator/air gunner
Sergeant M. T. Dower, RAAF, air gunner, survived, injured

Some 35 minutes into his first solo, early-evening, night-circuit detail on the Wellington, while flying the downwind leg, Flight Sergeant Westphal reported that an engine had cut. Almost instantly, however, he transmitted again, 'OK now.' His next call was 'Funnels'. This referred to a contemporary light-array positioning system, but effectively meant that he was lined up with the runway [or on finals]. In response to this he was given clearance to 'pancake' [land]. Evidently he then became dissatisfied with his approach – control noted that he was approaching rather steeply – for at some 150 feet he declared that he was going round again. The aircraft was heard to power up normally, but shortly after overflying the airfield it rapidly lost height, crashed 'near the local railway line' [the alabaster tramway], and burnt. Only Air Gunner Sergeant Dower survived.

Regrettably, the rear-crew survivor was unable to say whether the engine problem had re-occurred. He was, however, able to report that just before impact either the pilot or the air bomber, Flight Sergeant Miller, had announced on the intercom '100 on the clock', showing that, in the cockpit, the airspeed had been of prime concern. Unable to find a definite cause for the accident, therefore, the inquiry surmised that the flaps had been raised too early on the climb-out.

The reasoning here would have been that with lift-producing element of flap raised too soon, the pilot would have been faced with an invidious choice. He needed to achieve a safe flying speed. But the only way to do this was to lower the nose. The stalling speed, with flap, was of the order of 80 mph. Without flap, though, he needed 95 mph. The relieved announcement '100 mph on the clock', therefore, meant that they would have been safe, in free air. Only the fatal trade of height for speed had brought them irretrievably close to the ground.

It is noted, however, that the pupil was not directed to land at once, having reported an engine inexplicably cutting out (the procedural word 'Pancake' was not an imperative, but merely gave permission to land). And this makes the testimony of Mrs Ruth Russell (née Archer), now of Brookside Farm, but then a six-year old at the adjacent Brookhouse Farm, particularly relevant.

'It was dark, and all the adults were in the sheds, busy with the evening milking, so I was in the front room with my two young brothers. Suddenly there was this noise, and a glare through the window as a burning aeroplane passed between the house and hay barn.'

True, engines straining at full power are likely to emit flaring exhaust flames. But certainly, in this instance, it was the flare that drew the eye. There were no adult witnesses, and the inquiry did not question the children, but if, as seems possible, the troublesome engine had subsequently caught fire, then those in the cockpit would have had even more to distract them from the very demanding speed/height trade.

What was not taken as noteworthy, being the norm, was that Flight Sergeant Westphal had flown a total of just 171 hours, and only 33 on Wellingtons; 18 hours solo at night, but just the 40 minutes of that flight on Wellingtons. What did draw comment, however – though as a non-contributory fact – was that, in contradiction to orders for exercises involving overshooting and single-engined practice, the aircraft was carrying a full fuel load when, at the last, it had so desperately needed speed!

Regarding the accident card, it is not unusual of its type in that it inaccurately records both the crash location and the pilot's surname.

Mr Henry John Archer, of Brookhouse Farm, Ruth's brother, was taken to the site next day. 'We went through the gate at the end of Home Field,' he remembers, 'across the next culvert, twenty or so yards further on, and there it was, but largely burnt out. Though some years back enthusiasts found cartridges and debris scraps.'

Visiting the Site

A private track, alongside Home Field, leads the half mile from the farm to the site, for the most part paralleling the dismantled tramway which once brought alabaster from the local mine.

112 PERCIVAL PRENTICE P.40 (RAF T.1) VZ645 (SEE FIGS 162–163)
Foston Hall Woods

SK 18653 31041 (60 m)
Unit and Station: No. 16 Reserve Flying School, RAF Burnaston, Derby
Date: 5 March 1952
Crew: two, pilot and pupil, both killed
Flight Lieutenant Eric Church, RAFVR, instructor
Cadet Pilot Barbara Gubbins, WRAF Reserve

Flight Lieutenant Church's detail was to further familiarise his pupil with the complexities of spinning, essentially an out-of-control evolution. Contemporary rules demanded that practice spins should be entered at a minimum of 5,000 feet above ground level (AGL), the guidance (for elementary types) reading, 'when you have come down to 3,000 feet, you must prepare to abandon ... be sure ... that you can be out of the aircraft by 1,000 feet'. Despite this, some 17 minutes after take-off the aircraft was seen to be spinning, relatively flatly, at a layman's estimate of just 400 feet. Shortly afterwards the canopy was jettisoned and the pupil rose to her feet. Only moments later, though, the aircraft struck the ground, killing both occupants. Among the would-be rescuers were farm workers, and staff and lads from the nearby Scropton Hall Approved School (now Her Majesty's Women's Prison, Foston).
As no technical fault was found the court of enquiry had to conclude that the rules had been flouted and the spin recovery mishandled.

Flight Lieutenant Church had trained in the Reserve before the war, then served in Coastal Command, earning a mention in dispatches. Cadet Pilot Barbara Gubbins, an undergraduate at Nottingham University, had gained a private licence before joining the RAF Reserve. It is intriguing to consider that she might well have become the first woman to be awarded RAF wings, a distinction to be gained just six months later by Pilot Officer Jean Lennox Bird.

This was not to be the RAF's last spinning fatality, but certainly it helped raised awareness of this facet of flight safety, for shortly afterwards the rules would state unequivocally, 'If spin recovery action has not been effective by 3,000 feet AGL, abandon the aircraft.'

Visiting the Site

As might be expected, with such a light aircraft, the site being on farming land, and after such a passage of time, no sign of the tragedy remains. An abundance of woodland paths and tracks, however, mighty tempt the walker ...

PART THREE
APPENDICES

Appendix: Aircraft Types

This section aims to provide the moorland walker-reader with a (very) potted guide to the once-proud aircraft now represented, at best, by pools of debris. As for performance figures, published sources dealing with wartime aircraft often perpetuate values enhanced for propaganda purposes. But then even those quoted in *Pilot's Notes* incorporate a healthy safety margin, while flying any one of a line-up of a given aircraft type will show all such data to be merely representative. Then again, to avoid wearisome repetition, British aircraft invariably employed Browning, Lewis, or Vickers 0.303 inch (7.7 mm) calibre machine guns.

Airspeed Oxford
The 1937 twin-engined, wooden-framed, plywood-skinned Airspeed Oxford was a general-purpose trainer that had a basic crew of three but could accommodate other trainee-aircrew depending upon the role. Typically powered by two 375 horsepower Armstrong Siddeley Cheetah Ten radial engines, it had a maximum speed of 188 mph (163 knots), a cruising speed of 163 mph (142 knots), a ceiling of 19,000 feet and a range of 700 miles. It could carry practice bombs and a few had a dorsal (back-mounted) turret with a single machine gun.

Armstrong Whitworth Albemarle
With much wood and steel being used in its construction, the twin-engined, twin-finned, nominally four-crewed Albemarle saved on hard-to-procure light alloys and lent itself to sub-contracting. Among its forward-looking design features, it had a nosewheel-configuration undercarriage, yet between conception and construction it fell short of the updated requirements for a reconnaissance bomber and on coming into service in January 1943, it was relegated to the transport and glider-tug roles.

Powered by two 1,590 horsepower Bristol Hercules Eleven radial engines, the Albemarle cruised at some 170 mph (148 knots), had a ceiling of 18,000 feet and a range of 1,300 miles. It was armed with twin dorsally-mounted Vickers machine guns.

Armstrong Whitworth Whitley
This 1936 five-crewed, twin-engined bomber was withdrawn from Bomber Command operations in April 1942 but served on in the training, maritime, paratrooping, clandestine-operations, and glider-tug roles. Typically, two 1,145 horsepower Rolls-Royce Merlin in-line engines were fitted but performance figures – many subject to wartime propaganda – vary widely. Mid-road would be a cruising speed of 180 mph (156 knots) with a ceiling of 26,000 feet.

Typical armament was a single machine gun in the nose, and four in a tail turret. The bomb load was 7,000 pounds over a range of 1,500 miles.

Avro Anson

The 1935 Anson stayed with the RAF for twenty-two years. Originally conceived as a maritime reconnaissance aircraft, it was withdrawn from operational service in early 1942, after which it was employed extensively in the training role. As a dual-controlled machine with such innovations as hydraulically-operated flaps and undercarriage, it was used to train most aircrew specialisations. Normally accommodating between three and five, it could also be configured as an eight- to eleven-seat communications aircraft. It was well liked, being easy to fly, dependable, sturdy, and relatively forgiving. Its performance on one engine, however, was poor.

The Anson was typically powered by two 350 horsepower Armstrong Siddeley Cheetah Nine radial engines. These gave it a cruising speed of 158 mph (138 knots), a ceiling of 19,000 feet, and a range of nearly 800 miles.

Avro Lancaster

The Lancaster, a four-engined machine which metamorphosed from the twin-engined Manchester, became operational in 1942. Designed for ease of production and subsequent servicing, 7,737 were built by 1946.

With a normal crew complement of seven, and powered by four 1,640 horsepower Rolls-Royce Merlin Mk 24 engines, the Lancaster cruised at some 210 mph (182 knots) – or at 140 mph (122 knots) if reduced to three engines. It operated at up to 22,000 feet over a normal range of 2,500 miles. As defensive armament it had eight machine guns, four in the tail and two each in nose and dorsal turrets. The standard bomb load was 14,000 pounds or, having been modified, one 22,000-pound bomb. For a comparison often made, the Flying Fortress's standard bomb load was 6,000 pounds.

Avro Tutor

The Avro Tutor was the RAF's standard elementary trainer from 1932 until 1939. Formed of welded steel-tube construction covered with fabric, the machine was typically powered by a 240 horsepower Armstrong Siddeley Lynx Mk 4C radial engine screened by an aerodynamically enhancing Townend ring. It had a maximum speed of 122 mph (106 knots), cruised at 105 mph (91 knots), a range of 250 miles and a ceiling of 16,200 feet.

It was ahead of its age in having a self-centring tailwheel, adjustable seats and rudder pedals, a variable-incidence all-flying tailplane, and efficient brakes. It was also designed for ease of servicing.

In all, it seems, it was a gentleman's aircraft, and well liked, but if anything just a little too docile and forgiving for a trainer.

Bell 206B, Jet Ranger Helicopter

The publicity for the four- to six-seater Bell 206B Helicopter claimed, 'First in its class in safety, this aircraft ensures its crew will be back to fly another day.' A 400 shaft-horse-power Allison 250-C20 engine typically gave a top speed of 132 mph (115 knots), a cruising speed of 115 mph (100 knots), an endurance of three hours, and a range of 435 miles.

Boeing B-17 Flying Fortress

The perceived role of the 1935 Boeing B-17 was that of a long-range outpost capable of defending America beyond the range of its shore defences, hence 'Flying Fortress'. Testing on operations with the RAF showed that self-sealing fuel tanks and an increased amount of protective armour were necessary, after which it became the mainstay of the United States Eighth Army Air Force's bombing campaign.

The enormous tail fin ensured that it provided a stable bombing platform up to its 40,000-foot ceiling, while its formidable defensive armament and its capacity for absorbing battle damage was held to compensate for its relatively small bomb load.

The upgraded B-17G version relied for its defence on up to thirteen 0.5 inch (12.7 mm), heavy-calibre machine guns, this firepower being enhanced by the formation strategies employed. With so many guns to man, the standard crew complement was ten. This comprised pilot, co-pilot, navigator, bombardier, flight engineer, and radio operator. In combat the flight engineer would man the top turret, and the wireless operator the dorsal turret. The remaining four crew were dedicated gunners to man the ball-turret, the left and right waist positions, and the tail turret.

The B-17 was typically powered by four 1,200 horsepower Wright Cyclone R-1820-65 9-cylinder air-cooled engines which, with Hamilton three-bladed, constant-speed, fully-feathering propellers, gave it a cruising speed of 225 mph (196 knots). It had a normal range of 3,000 miles and a standard bomb load of 6,000 pounds, although this could be increased to 12,800 pounds, and over a very short range, to 20,800 pounds.

Bristol Blenheim

In 1935 the prototype Blenheim proved faster than any fighter. By 1939, however, it was outclassed by most German types but, although swiftly withdrawn from bombing operations, it served on as a radar-equipped night-fighter, and later as an advanced crew trainer.

Two 905 horsepower Bristol Mercury Fifteen radial engines gave a representative Blenheim a ceiling of 27,000 feet, a cruising speed of 198 mph (172 knots) and a range of 1,460 miles.

Armed with two machine guns in a power-operated dorsal turret, with two remotely controlled guns below the nose and a fifth in the port wing, it could also carry a 1,300-pound load of bombs.

Bristol Bulldog

The 1927 Bristol Bulldog biplane fighter had an all-metal, fabric-covered airframe and was typically powered by a 440 horsepower Bristol Jupiter radial engine. This gave it a maximum speed of 174 mph (151 knots), a time to 20,000 feet of fifteen minutes and a ceiling of 27,000 feet. It was armed with two fixed Vickers machine guns synchronised to fire through the propeller, and could also carry four 20 pound bombs in underwing racks.

The Mark 2 version entered RAF service in mid-1929 and was equipped with oxygen and a radio transmitter.

Bristol Fighter Mk 3

The 1916 Bristol Fighter Mk 2B – from the outset 'Fighter', and never 'Scout' – reached the Western Front in April 1917. It had a disastrous baptism of fire, but once the Royal Flying Corps learnt to use it as an offensive, rather than a defensive machine, it became a telling force. After the war the RAF adopted the type as the standard army co-operation machine, and in 1926 all restructured Mk 2s were re-designated Mk 3s.

A 275 horsepower Rolls-Royce Falcon 3 engine gave the wooden-framed, two-seater biplane a maximum speed of 123 mph (107 knots), a time to 10,000 feet of twelve minutes, a ceiling of 20,000 feet, and an endurance of three hours. Its touchdown speed was 45 mph (39 knots).

It carried a synchronised Vickers machine gun firing through the propeller, and at least one Lewis mounted on a Scarff Ring in the rear cockpit; additionally, it could carry 240 pounds of bombs. It was withdrawn from service in 1932.

Consolidated-Vultee 32 Liberator

Other designations: United States Army, B-24 Liberator; RAF, Liberator

The late-1939 long-range B-24 Liberator was immediately ordered by Britain and France, with Britain inheriting the whole order when France fell. The type was first used by the British Overseas Airways

Corporation and Coastal Command. However, by September 1943 the Americans themselves had come to appreciate its value. Over 18,000 were built, with the production rate reaching one every fifty-six minutes.

Four 1,200 horsepower Pratt & Whitney Twin Wasp engines driving Curtiss three-bladed, electrically-driven, constant-speed propellers gave a cruising speed of 220 mph (191 knots) and a ceiling of 36,000 feet. The range was 2,500 miles and the bomb load 8,000 pounds. Armament was up to fourteen machine guns of 0.5 inch (12.7 mm) calibre, in four turrets and two waist positions.

Desoutter Mk 1
The Desoutter Mk I was a British licence-built version of the Dutch-designed Koolhoven FK41, a three-seater monoplane. Between 1929 and 1931 it was built by Desoutter Aircraft at Croydon and used, primarily by National Flying Services at Hanworth, in the instructional, taxi, and pleasure-flying roles. Some were used as ambulances.

Typically powered by a 115 horsepower Hermes Mk 2 engine, it had a maximum speed of 115 mph (99 knots).

De Havilland DH60G Gipsy Moth
The first of the two-seater, single-engined Moth biplane family made its initial flight in February 1925. The 1928 DH60G Gipsy Moth was an early development. A 100 horsepower Gipsy engine gave a maximum speed of 105 mph (91 knots), a cruising speed of 85 mph (74 knots) and a ceiling of 18,000 feet. The Moth's range was some 300 miles.

De Havilland Hornet
The 1944 Hornet, conceived as a single-seater, long-range fighter for use in the Pacific theatre, was one of several private designs by de Havilland. Longer and slimmer than the Mosquito, with 'handed' propellers to obviate torque, it was deployed in both the UK and the Far East.

Powered by two 2,030 horsepower Rolls-Royce Merlin in-line engines, it had a maximum speed of 472 mph (410 knots), a ceiling of 37,500 feet, and a range of 2,500 miles when using drop tanks. It mounted four 20 mm calibre cannon in the nose, and carried 2,000 pounds of bombs or rockets.

Although too late to see action in the Second World War, the Hornet did become operational in Malaya, its final version being the RAF's fastest-ever piston-engined fighter.

De Havilland Mosquito
The 1940 private-venture Mosquito, the two-seated, twin-engined 'Wooden Wonder', was an instant success with both the Service and the war-jaded public. First conceived as a fast, high-flying bomber that would need no performance-limiting defensive armament, the authorities had only tardily recognised its potential, the machine owing virtually everything to the faith of the de Havilland company.

The wooden construction was light, and saved on scarce alloys, while the 1,620 horsepower Rolls-Royce Merlin 25 in-line engines gave a cruising speed of 325 mph (283 knots) and a ceiling of 33,000 feet. The Mosquito had a range of 1,650 miles.

It proved itself the master of many roles: photo reconnaissance, bomber, intruder, fighter-bomber, night-fighter, and communications-cum-freighter, and passing through many variants, remained in service until 1961. With pilot and navigator seated side by side, the armed versions typically carried four 20 mm calibre cannon and four machine guns in the nose. Its bomb load was 2,000 pounds.

De Havilland Puss Moth
One of the de Havilland biplane series, the Puss Moth's enclosed cabin generally seated two in tandem, but was capable of carrying three.

A 130 horsepower de Havilland Gipsy Major engine gave a maximum speed of 128 mph (111 knots), a cruising speed of 105 mph (91 knots), a range of 300 miles and a ceiling of 17,500 feet. Singularly, the undercarriage strut could be turned through ninety degrees to act as an airbrake.

De Havilland DH82A Tiger Moth
The 1934 tandem two-seater biplane de Havilland trainer was used at over eighty wartime elementary flying training schools. A 130 horsepower de Havilland Gipsy Major in-line engine gave it a cruising speed of 93 mph (80 knots), a ceiling of 13,000 feet and a range of 300 miles. To maintain the centre of gravity a solo pilot sat in the rear seat. Although demanding to fly accurately, and invariably giving a freezing cold ride, the Tiger Moth had no vices.

De Havilland Venom FB (fighter-bomber)
The 1949 twin-boomed, single-seater de Havilland Venom was a far more sophisticated design than the Vampire it succeeded. This enabled it to take advantage of the higher Mach numbers its more powerful Ghost engine could propel it to. Equipping many squadrons in the mid-50s, it won praise for its rate of climb and its manoeuvrability at high altitudes. The 1953 variant had an ejection seat.

Of all-metal, stressed-skin construction, the Venom was powered by a 4,850 pounds thrust de Havilland Ghost 103 engine which gave it a maximum speed of 597 mph (519 knots), a rate of climb of 7,230 feet a minute, a ceiling of 48,000 feet, and a range of 1,075 miles. It had four 20 mm calibre guns in the nose and could carry 2,000 pounds of bombs.

Douglas C-47 Skytrain, RAF Dakota
The 1935 Douglas DC-3, basically carrying twenty-one passengers and a crew of three, the doyen of air transports, was still flying commercially in 2012. One of its many variants, the C-47 Skytrain, with a strengthened floor and wide cargo hatch, proved adaptable to a seemingly infinite number of tasks.

Two 1,050 horsepower Pratt & Whitney Twin Wasp air-cooled engines gave it a cruising speed of 207 mph (180 knots) and a ceiling of 23,200 feet. It had 2,125 miles' range and a stalling speed of 67 mph (58 knots).

Douglas C-53 Skytrooper, RAF Dakota Mk 2
The Douglas C-53 Skytrooper was the first military version of the DC-3 airliner, with up to twenty-eight fully armed parachute troops being seated in fixed metal seats arranged along the fuselage. An alternative fit was twenty-four stretchers and it was also employed as a glider-tug. The narrow door of the civil airliner was retained, while neither the floor nor the undercarriage were reinforced.

Typically powered by two 1,000 horsepower Wright Cyclone radial engines, it had a maximum speed of 220 mph (191 knots), a cruising speed of 194 mph (169 knots), a stalling speed of 67 mph (58 knots), and a ceiling of 21,900 feet. Its range was 2,125 miles.

English Electric Canberra
The 1949 Canberra, conceived as a replacement for the de Havilland Mosquito, entered RAF service in May 1951 and was to remain in use until the turn of the century, passing through some thirty different versions.

Reasonably typical performance figures based on two Rolls-Royce Avon engines, each of 11,000 pounds thrust, gave the Canberra a maximum speed of 517 mph (449 knots), an initial climb rate of 3,400 feet a minute and a ceiling of 48,000 feet. It had a combat range of 805 miles and ferry range of 3,600 miles. It could carry 6,000 pounds of ordnance.

The photo-reconnaissance (PR) Canberra flew unarmed, relying upon speed and altitude to protect it. In both bomber and PR roles it was crewed by a pilot and two navigators, with one of the latter operating the specialist equipment.

Europa Kit Aeroplane

The Europa kit aeroplane, fabricated at Kirkbymoorside, quickly built up a reputation for being dependable and enjoyable to fly. A two-seat composite monoplane whose various adaptations included a glider-wing fit, it could be swiftly de-rigged for transportation on a trailer and storage in a garage.

A Rotax 80 or 100 horsepower engine gave it a 138 to 161 mph (120 to 140 knots) speed range.

Gloster Meteor

The 1943 Meteor was the only Allied jet aircraft to see service during the Second World War. Developmental delays, however, meant that the RAF only received it in July 1944. After that, armed with four 20 mm calibre cannon, the twin-jet fighter was successfully deployed against the V1 Flying Bombs. Variants and modifications included a two-seater trainer and a two-crew night-fighter, also the provision of Martin Baker ejection seats.

Early versions were powered by two Rolls-Royce Welland turbojet engines, each developing 1,700 pounds of static thrust, to give a top speed of 415 mph (361 knots) and a ceiling of 40,000 feet. Later versions, fitted with the more powerful Rolls-Royce Derwent 8 engines, each giving 3,660 pounds of thrust, brought the speed up to nearly 600 mph (521 knots). The type was phased out of service in the 1960s.

Handley Page Halifax

The 1940, seven-crewed, twin-finned Halifax heavy bomber found favour with its versatility, for besides its design role it was employed in both the transport and maritime roles, also as an ambulance, a glider tug, and as a clandestine and paratroop-delivery vehicle.

Typically, four 1,615 horsepower Bristol Hercules Sixteen radial engines gave it a cruising speed of 215 mph (187 knots) and a ceiling of 24,000 feet. It had a range of 1,030 miles and could carry 13,000 pounds of bombs. It mounted nine machine guns, one in the nose, and four each in dorsal and tail turrets.

An unfortunate characteristic of early Halifaxes was that fully-laden aircraft could enter an inverted, and effectively uncontrollable, spin. A retrospective modification of the tailfin leading-edge shape from triangular to quadrilateral helped overcome this stability defect.

Hawker Hart

In air exercises the 1930 Hawker Hart bomber easily outstripped the latest fighters, so acting as a spur to the RAF's re-equipment. It was only in late 1939 that it was replaced by Harvards and Masters; as a consequence, many distinguished Second World War pilots got their wings on the type.

Typically, a 525 horsepower Rolls-Royce Kestrel engine gave a maximum speed of 184 mph (160 knots), a cruise of 145 mph (126 knots), a range of 430 miles, and a ceiling of 22,800 feet.

Hawker Hurricane

In 1933, when Hawkers conceived this celebrated monoplane fighter, the British authorities were still suspicious of all but biplanes, a prejudice dating back to the failure of one of Monsieur Blériot's monoplane designs in 1912. The Blériot problem had been swiftly solved, but two subsequent British monoplane crashes, none of the three in the least connected, had led to the British Army – but not the Royal Navy – banning all its pilots from flying monoplanes. Indeed, it was Hawkers, rather than Authority, who ensured that by the outbreak of the Second World War the RAF had nineteen Hurricane squadrons.

That more Hurricanes than Spitfires fought in the Battle of Britain is well known, but both types, being of such sound design, underwent constant modification. Typically, however, a 1,280 horsepower Rolls-Royce Merlin Twenty in-line engine gave a maximum speed of 342 mph (297 knots), a cruising speed of 296 mph (257 knots), an initial climb rate of 2,700 feet a minute, and a ceiling of 36,500 feet. The Hurricane had a range of 480 miles, or 985 miles with external fuel tanks, and carried twelve forward-firing, wing-mounted machine guns, together with a 500-pound bomb load.

Heinkel He 111

The 1935 Heinkel He 111 (one-eleven) was blooded with the Condor Legion in the Spanish Civil War, and later in Poland, handsomely outstripping the opposing fighters. Over Britain, however, both its armament and performance proved inadequate, particularly as German fighters were unable to dwell long enough to provide meaningful support. From mid-September 1940, therefore, it was restricted to night-time operations.

Two 1100 Junkers Jumo engines gave an average speed (collating various sources) of 250 mph (217 knots), a ceiling of 23,000 feet, and a range of 1,030 miles. Early versions had a crew of four, a bomb load of some 4,000 pounds, and armament comprising three 7.9 mm calibre machine guns mounted dorsally, in the nose, and in a belly turret.

Hughes 369E Helicopter

The 1963 Hughes 369/500 series Helicopter, adapted from an American Army requirement, passed through many versions. Typically, however, it seated five and, powered by a 420 horsepower turboshaft Allison engine, had a speed range from hover to 180 mph (156 knots), a range of some 260 miles, and a ceiling of 12,500 feet. Rugged and reliable, it was said to possess crisp handling qualities and to be highly manoeuvrable.

The aircraft in this volume, G-OABG, was fitted, among other things, with both an automatic pilot and a moving-map global positioning navigational system.

Junkers Ju 88

Fortunately for the Allies, German aircraft designers, like their British counterparts, frequently had changes forced upon them. So although the 1939 Junkers Ju 88 bomber was envisaged as a fast, minimally-armed machine capable of targeting the whole of the British Isles, the Luftwaffe's insistence that it be used primarily as a dive bomber called for a more robust construction. This increased the weight and reduced the design speed and manoeuvrability, reductions which called for more defensive armament. The bitter pill for its adherents was that it was never actually used as a dive-bomber except when operating over water!

The type was adapted to many roles but two 1,400 horsepower Junkers 211J liquid-cooled inverted V12 engines typically gave a maximum speed of 295 mph (256 knots) and a ceiling of 26,900 feet. A crew of four comprised pilot, bomb aimer, top-gunner/radio-operator and lower-gunner/flight-engineer. Armament was a 7.9 mm calibre gun under the control of the pilot, and three 7.9 mm calibre guns and a 13 mm calibre gun fought by the gunners. Four 1,000-kilogram bombs could be carried.

Lockheed P-38 Lightning

The 1939 Lockheed P-38 Lightning fighter, twin-engined and twin-boomed, had a range that could be extended to 3,000 miles using auxiliary tanks, enabling fleets of P-38s to make the Atlantic crossing under their own steam. This extended range was to be equally valued by the deeply-penetrating American bomber crews who, by 1943, were suffering increasingly from a lack of fighter support. Ground troops also gained from the superior endurance of the P-38, which could dwell and give support for an hour longer than other fighters.

Powered by a 1,090 horsepower Allison V-1710 12-cylinder Prestone-cooled engine, driving a three-bladed Curtiss electric constant-speed, fully-feathering propeller, the type had a typical top speed of over 400 mph (348 knots), cruised at 300 mph (261 knots), had an initial rate of climb of 2,850 feet a minute and a ceiling of 40,000 feet.

Typical armament was a 20 mm cannon and four 0.5 inch calibre machine guns in the nose, with a bomb load of 2,000 pounds.

Mignet Flying Flea

The 1934 Flying Flea was a build-it-yourself aeroplane, designed by Frenchman Henri Mignet and introduced in his book, *Le Pou-du-Ciel*. Mignet claimed for the Flea, 'With an instructor I'd have been a pilot at the end of five minutes.' And women? 'The woman?' he wrote, 'Her light weight (don't make me say her small brain) invites her particularly to the sport of the air!'

Flea construction became a craze, but there were so many crashes – and some fatalities – that by 1937 the Flea had been banned in both France and Britain.

Mignet's 1934 claim was that an Aubier-Dunne 20 horsepower engine driving a five-foot diameter propeller gave a cruise of 65 mph (56 knots). The Flea took off in 300 feet and landed in 175 feet after an approach at 19 mph (17 knots). And the ceiling? After ten hours' test flying, Mignet had not found out, explaining, 'It has been too cold. But … call it 10,000 feet if you will. It is quite enough to fly over a lot of clouds.'

Miles Magister

The 1936 tandem-seated, low-winged, metal-skinned Miles Hawk monoplane so impressed the RAF that a Service version, the Magister elementary trainer, was ordered. Powered by a 130 horsepower de Havilland Gipsy Major One in-line engine, it had a cruising speed of 123 mph (107 knots), a ceiling of 18,000 feet, and a range of 380 miles. It boasted wheelbrakes, power-operated flaps, and a tailwheel – as opposed to a skid – and could be flown solo from either seat, although the front seat was preferred.

Unlike its contemporary, the Tiger Moth, it responded well in gusty conditions. On the other hand, unless controlled, the Hawk's wing would lift markedly in a crosswind. Then again, there were trimming controls to master. These were just two of the 'complications' that made it a good trainer. And there were no vices. Only, for all its good points, it never aroused anything like the affection engendered by the Tiger Moth.

Miles Master Mk 1

In the late 1930s it was realised that pupils would find it a daunting undertaking to step from Tiger Moths and Magisters into the new, high-performance Spitfires and Hurricanes. The 1937 Miles Kestrel, a private venture, seemed to be the answer, being just twenty miles an hour slower than the Hurricane. However, in adopting it the Ministry called for so many modifications that in March 1939, when the emergent Miles Master trainer actually flew, it had dropped nearly a hundred miles an hour. The saving grace was that the tandem-seat trainer had handling characteristics similar to those of the new fighters, in that respect, at least, easing the transition from trainer to first-line fighter.

The Master Mk 1 was powered by a 715 horsepower Kestrel Mk 30 in-line engine which gave it a maximum speed of 226 mph (196 knots), a ceiling of 28,000 feet, and a range of 500 miles.

The Master Mk 3 first flew in 1940. Powered by an 825 horsepower Pratt & Whitney Wasp Junior radial engine, it had a maximum speed of 232 mph (202 knots) and a cruising speed of 170 mph (148 knots) while retaining the 85 mph (74 knots) landing speed of the Mk 1s and Mk 2s.

North American Harvard

The 1935 Harvard advanced trainer was ordered by both France and Britain, over a hundred being delivered to France before it fell. An untimely delivery, for the Luftwaffe then used them for training and also for familiarising pilots who were tasked to evaluate captured American machines. The Harvard served the RAF from 1939 until 1955, but was to remain in the South African Air Force until 1995.

Typically, a 550/600 horsepower, 9-cylinder Pratt & Whitney Wasp engine, air-cooled, and driving a Hamilton two-bladed, two-position controllable-pitch propeller, gave a top speed of 206 mph (179 knots) and a cruising speed of 180 mph (156 knots). The landing speed was 63 mph (55 knots), the ceiling 23,000 feet, and the range 730 miles. Although popular, it was a demanding machine – and therefore, a good advanced trainer.

Percival Prentice T.1
This 1946 all-metal basic pilot trainer, with two seats side by side, replaced the Tiger Moth and Magister amd was supplanted by the piston Provost. Powered by a 251 horsepower de Havilland Gypsy Queen 32, it had a service ceiling of 18,000 feet, cruised at 136 mph (118 knots) and had a maximum speed of 143 mph (124 knots).

Republic P-47 Thunderbolt
Republic's 1941 P-47 Thunderbolt high-altitude, medium- to long-range escort fighter began operating in Europe in early 1943 and quickly proved its worth. Indeed, from March 1944, with its range extended by droppable tanks, it was able to escort the bombers on round-trip raids upon Berlin.

The Thunderbolt was typically powered by a 2,000 horsepower turbo-supercharged Pratt & Whitney Double Wasp air-cooled engine driving a four-bladed Curtiss constant-speed, fully-feathering propeller. This combination gave it a maximum speed of some 433 mph (376 knots), an initial climb rate of 2,805 feet a minute, a ceiling of over 40,000 feet, and a range greater than 1,700 miles.

It was armed with eight wing-mounted 0.5 inch calibre machine guns and could also fire rocket projectiles or deliver two 1,000-pound bombs from underwing mountings.

Short Stirling
The Short Stirling, the first of the RAF's heavy bombers, came into service in 1941. Shorts re-used their successful Sunderland wing profile but Ministry requirements limited the span to 100 feet (not, as myth has it, to fit into RAF hangars, which were 125 feet wide). This, and similar modifications, detracted from the design performance, giving the Stirling a ceiling of only 17,000 feet. It was, however, very manoeuvrable, and powered by four 1,650 horsepower Bristol Hercules Sixteen radial engines, had a maximum speed of 270 mph (235 knots), a cruise of 200 mph (174 knots) and a range – dependent upon bomb load – of up to 2,000 miles. Its cockpit stood at a lofty 22 feet 9 inches above the tarmac.

The Stirling carried 14,000 pounds of bombs and had eight machine guns, four in a tail turret, and two each in nose and dorsal turrets.

It was popular with its seven- or eight-man crews but its bomb bay could not be adapted as bigger bombs were developed and it ceased bomber operations in September 1941. It was then very successfully employed in the glider-tug, clandestine-operations, and transport roles. A dedicated transport variant was also developed, 160 examples being built.

Stinson Reliant
The Stinson Reliant 'Gullwing', a rugged four- to five-seater constructed of fabric-covered welded steel, was an aircraft ideally suited to the contact flying carried out by the RAF's Army Cooperation and Camouflage units. It was easy to handle in the air: a boon for the pilot, who was required to fly low while devoting most of his attention to what was going on outside and below the aircraft. Further to which, its built-in stability was claimed to allow it to recover 'hands-off' from any inadvertent stall.

A 300 horsepower Lycoming R600 engine gave it a cruising speed of some 130 mph (113 knots) and a ceiling of 15,600 feet. It had a range of at least 700 miles and an endurance of five hours. It required a run of 780 feet for take-off, 700 feet for landing. Its clean stalling speed of 65 mph (56 knots) reduced to 56 mph (50 knots) with flap.

Supermarine Seafire
The Hurricane having been successfully adapted to a carrier-role, it was natural that the Royal Navy's attention should turn to the Spitfire, only to find that its narrow-track undercarriage caused deck-landing problems. Just the same, hook-adapted Spitfire Mark Fives were developed as Seafire 1Bs, the variant Seafire Mk 3 having folding wings.

In truth, the Seafire was never entirely suited to carrier operations; in particular, its propeller tips would strike the deck as the aircraft pitched nose-down on being arrested, a problem which was resolved in pragmatic Royal Navy style by clipping six inches off the end of all Seafire propellers as a matter of course.

Representative Seafire performance was a maximum speed of 352 mph (306 knots), a cruising speed of 218 mph (189 knots), a ceiling of 33,800 feet, and a range of 465 miles, or 725 with a drop tank.

Supermarine Spitfire

Like his opposite numbers in Hawkers, the Spitfire's designer, R. J. Mitchell, had to fight the prejudice against monoplane machines. Fortunately, as with the Hurricane, the Ministry was persuaded to accept Mitchell's design, and the Spitfire duly came into being in early 1936. It would metamorphose through over a score of variant Marks, but performance figures for the early marks should suffice here.

The 1938 Spitfire Mark 1 was powered by a 1,030 horsepower Rolls-Royce Merlin Mark Two in-line engine, driving a two-bladed, wooden, fixed-pitch propeller. This combination gave a maximum speed of about 350 mph (304 knots) and a cruising speed of some 265 mph (230 knots). The undercarriage and flaps had to be manually operated, however, and due to supply difficulties, only four of the planned eight machine guns were installed. None of this would give a complete picture, however, unless the superb handling qualities of the machine were mentioned from the start.

Technical modifications began almost at once, including the provision of armoured plating behind the engine, a bullet-proof windscreen, and a metal, three-bladed, variable-pitched propeller. And with the missing four guns added, the designation was changed to the Mark 1A.

The Mark 2 Spitfire was given a 1,175 horsepower Rolls-Royce Merlin Twelve engine, the Mark 2A development retaining the eight machine guns of the original design.

Modifications would continue throughout the Second World War, in turn befitting the Spitfire to any task that could be asked of a single-seat fighter, production ending in October 1947.

Vickers Varsity T Mk 1

The Vickers Varsity T Mk 1 was a mid-wing, stressed-skin, twin-engined crew-training aircraft. In Service use throughout the 1950s and 1960s, the Varsity was well liked by those who flew it. Sturdy, dependable, a stable instrument-flying platform, and handy on one engine – safely climbing at 132 mph (115 knots) with an engine out – it was also a generously forgiving aircraft, besides which its nosewheel-configured undercarriage made it very straightforward to land. It had a dual-position bomb-aimer's station in a nacelle hung beneath the nose, and was used by the RAF for both pilot and rear-crew training. After its tenure of service ended in 1976, some Varsities passed into private hands.

Powered by two Hercules 264 Engines driving Rotal Hydromatic, fully-feathering propellers, it cruised at 239 mph (208 knots), had a maximum permitted speed of 288 mph (250 mph), a service ceiling of 28,700 feet, and a range of 2,648 miles.

Vickers Wellington

Because Wellington Operational Training Units abounded in the White Peak, it is understandable that the type should figure largely in this book. However, this merely reflects the intensity of training carried out and takes no account of the vast number of Wellington sorties accomplished entirely without incident.

The Germans quickly took the measure of the Wellingtons, after which the type was switched to night bombing. Additionally, it was constantly employed in the maritime role, using metal coils to detonate magnetic mines, and locating submarines with the aid of Air-to-Surface-Vessel radar (ASV) and Leigh searchlights.

The crew of four or five comprised a pilot, a navigator/bomb aimer (or a navigator and a bomb aimer), a wireless operator/air gunner, and an air gunner in the rear turret. Then again, on training sorties the machine would regularly carry six, swelled by a pilot instructor – even early Wellingtons might have a second, rather rudimentary set of flight controls – and specialist instructors for other trainees.

The Wellington was typically powered by two 1,500 horsepower Bristol Hercules Eleven radial engines that gave it a maximum speed of 235 mph (204 knots) and a ceiling of 19,000 feet. As for a representative cruising speed, choose your source, although a former Wellington pilot at Weybridge proposed 173 mph (150 knots). Additionally, he suggested a normal bombing altitude of 12,000 feet.

Certainly, the Wellington had a 4,500-pound bomb load and carried eight machine guns, two in a tail turret, two in the beam, and two in the nose. It continued in service until 1953, using the T.10 version dedicated to the pilot and navigator training roles with the nose turret faired over.

Vickers Warwick

Intended as an upgrade to the Wellington, the Warwick proved disappointing but was used in the maritime role. Similar in appearance to the Wellington, and just 'ten feet bigger all around', they could easily be mistaken for one another.

Westland Lysander

The 1936 Lysander was a purpose-designed, two-seater army co-operation machine delivered to the RAF in 1938. Although some saw action prior to the fall of France, the use of First World War techniques and the fact that the enemy had air superiority meant that losses were inordinately high. Accordingly, the type was rapidly withdrawn from such service but continued to serve as a target tug, and in the air-defence-co-operation and air-sea rescue roles. The Lysander excelled, however, as a clandestine delivery machine for the Special Operations Executive (SOE), where its short-field performance was well suited to landing supplies and personnel in occupied Europe.

With its cockpit standing fourteen and a half feet above the ground, the Lysander was typically powered by an 870 horsepower Bristol Mercury Twenty or Thirty radial engine that gave it a maximum speed of 212 mph (184 knots) and a ceiling of 21,500 feet. It had a range of 600 miles.

PART FOUR

Glossary

AAF: RAF stations taken over by the United States Army Air Force were designated by the initials AAF (American Air Force) and a number, so that RAF Burtonwood, near Liverpool, became AAF590.

Abeam: lying at right angles to the line of march. All things being equal, if an established path is followed until a site is directly off one's shoulder, then the least amount of rough walking is required to reach that site.

Air bomber: bomb aimer. The preferred term was bomb aimer.

Air-accident reports: the plethora of paperwork generated by RAF accidents was summarised on the card-indexed RAF Form 1180 (often hand-written), those still extant being held by the RAF Museum, Hendon. A generic failing is the imprecision of crash locations, a working reference having been sufficient to peg the report.

Aircrew: on 19 January 1939, non-commissioned aircrew (gunners) were effectively afforded the status of sergeants, although the situation was not regularised until early 1940, when heavy bombers appeared. Second World War aircrew categories comprised: pilot; navigator [observer, pre-1942]; wireless operator/ air gunner; air gunner; flight engineer [post-1941]; bomb aimer/air bomber [post-1942]. This omits the navigator/wireless operator category, and several similar combinations involving navigators.

Aircrew ranks (immediately post-war): There was a short-lived post-war attempt to reconcile aircrew status with that of ground-staff in the RAF, wartime aircrew having been accorded 'immediate' senior NCO status, in contrast to the slow promotion rate of non-flying personnel. However, the 'Aircrew-Rank' system, under which, for example, a sergeant pilot became a 'Pilot Grade Two' (P2), was scrapped again in 1950, only the Master-Aircrew title being retained.

Air Defence of Great Britain Command: an inter-war formation that was resurrected from 15 November 1943 until 15 October 1944 when it became Fighter Command once more.

Alabaster tramway: a narrow-gauge light railway which delivered gypsum alabaster from several mines near Scropton to the main railway. During the Second World War it was also used to take bombs from the underground store at Fauld.

Bar (to a gallantry award): this term indicates a further award of a gallantry decoration and is represented by a rosette sewn to the ribbon. Not to be confused with the 'medal bar' or 'medal clasp' (denoting campaigns) running across the ribbon of a general service medal.

Bearings and fixes (radio): in essence, a bearing taken across track would show how far along track an aircraft had reached, while the intersection of bearings from two stations 'fixed' the aircraft's position. With radio silence imposed, bearings could be obtained by directional loop. Otherwise ground direction-finding stations could be asked for bearings.

Blacking out (see also 'g' below): in a tight turn, centrifugal force pushes an airman into his seat. But his blood, too, is forced down, the resultant reduction of blood pressure in the head, not least in the eyeballs, leading to 'grey out', then to a total loss of vision known as 'black out', and unconsciousness.

Captain Lamplugh: when the British Aviation Insurance Company came into being in 1931 (Global
  Aerospace, in 2012), Captain A. G. Lamplugh, CBE, FRAeS, MIAeE, FRGS became the chief
  underwriter and principal surveyor. His oft-reproduced quote came from a paper – *Accidents in Civil
  Aviation* – he read to the Royal Aeronautical Society on 29 October 1931.

Circuits and Rollers: circuits and landings involved taking off into wind and climbing to some 1,000 feet,
  turning downwind parallel to the runway to fly past the airfield (the downwind leg), then turning back onto
  the final approach, touching down, rolling to a stop, and clearing the runway. Circuits and rollers – or bumps
  – required the pilot to touch down but then to smartly reconfigure the aircraft for flight, put on full power,
  and take off again. Circuits and overshoots required the pilot to power up on the final approach and climb
  away, as if the landing had been balked.

Darky: an emergency homing system making a benefit of the mere 25-mile range of wartime voice-radio
  sets. A listening station could give its own location, so advising a calling aircraft that it was within 25
  miles, often enough information to allow the lost crew to restart their own navigation. Conversely, the
  aircraft could be directed towards adjacent listening stations and so be led towards the nearest suitable
  airfield.

  The Royal Observer Corps proudly claimed that Darky saved over 7,000 lost Allied aircraft, with 1,800
  other damaged machines being guided to safe landings.

Degrees magnetic: measuring a track on the map will give the true direction. Adding five degrees will give
  the direction to set on the compass. So, a measured track of 070° is set on the compass ring as 075°.
  (Purists – and enthusiasts – will blanch, but the rest of us will be tramping heather for no more than
  half a mile or so.)

Dorsal (turret): a turret mounted on the top – the back – of the aircraft.

Feather: to electrically or hydraulically turn the blades of a stopped propeller edge-on to the airflow to cut
  down the drag, as with an oar in rowing. The propeller of a failed engine left blade-on to the airflow, and
  therefore said to be 'windmilling', creates an inordinate amount of drag.

Forced-landing/precautionary landing: a forced-landing is a set-down caused by a malfunction that gives
  the pilot no option but to alight. A precautionary landing is one where the pilot decides that it is politic
  to put down, so permitting the choice of a suitable site.

'g': acceleration due to gravity. Any high acceleration manoeuvre – change of direction, effectively – results
  in a change of weight, or of centrifugal force, which is categorised as measuring so many 'g'.

Geodetic: the structure developed by aircraft designer Sir Barnes Wallis and employed in the Wellington
  bomber. Essentially, it comprised triangular grids made up of aluminium strips to form a mutually
  supporting shell of great strength. More properly, the component parts formed 'geodetic' curves (parts of
  a circle) on the structure, each element taking the shortest line across the curved surface.

Ginnel: dialect, a narrow passage.

GPS: global positioning system. The satellite navigation system is essentially an American military facility
  that was opened to civilians in 1983 after an airliner was shot down on straying into a prohibited area. In
  2000, accuracy for civilian usage was markedly improved. Like a map and compass, however, a GPS repays
  study, after which it can be of inestimable value on the moor.

Gremlins: manikins whose *raison d'être* was to harass aircrew by creating technical problems. They appeared
  in 1940, got into print in the *RAF Journal* in 1942, indoctrinated fighter pilot Roald Dahl a little later and
  subsequently Walt Disney. They were known to be 'green, gamboge and gold; male, female and neuter;
  and both young and old', yet there were fliers who thought them fictitious.

Identity Disc: British personnel were issued with two. The green/brown (1916-issue) octagon-lozenge-shaped
  disc (35mm by 30mm) of vulcanised asbestos fibre was to be worn around the neck on a string and left
  with the body. The circular (35 mm diameter) red/brown disc (the 1914-issue, original disc), of identical
  fibre, was to be secured to the other by a separate string and removed for record purposes. Hand-stamped

and recording name, number, service, and religion, the issue was stabilised in 1920. The Americanism 'Dog tag' was not used during the period.

Mach number: named for the Austrian physicist Ernst Mach (1838–1916), this refers to the speed of an aircraft in relation to the speed of sound. So, an aircraft moving at twice the speed of sound travels at Mach 2, one at just 0.95 of sonic speed, Mach 0.95.

Ministry of Defence: created in 1971. Formerly, responsibilities in the matter of crash sites lay with the Air Ministry and the Ministry of Aircraft Production (later, Supply). The existence of the Protection of Military Remains Act 1986, order 2008, has to be acknowledged, but although this forbids unauthorised tampering with crash-sites it says nothing of Authority's moral responsibility for the countryside.

Mission (terminology): throughout the era embracing the Second World War, offensive flights against the enemy were termed missions by the United States Army Air Force and operational sorties – or Ops – by their RAF counterparts. The standard operational tour required from RAF crews may be taken as thirty. It is of note that in 2012 modern usage has the RAF flying missions (that similarly, wounded personnel are injured, and stations are bases).

'Queen Mary': the 1938-designed Tasker semi-trailer, aircraft-recovery combination was a 12-inch ground-clearance low loader, typically 33 feet long and capable of carrying 5 tons.

Special Operations Executive (SOE): an organisation of volunteers set up in July 1940 to carry out sabotage and subversion behind enemy lines. Churchill described its purpose as being to 'set Europe ablaze'.

Spin: essentially, a spin is a stalled condition of flight during which the aircraft descends in a spiral at a relatively low speed; this is an out-of-control evolution not to be confused with an increasing-speed spiral dive. Pilots investigate spins primarily to avoid entering them inadvertently. By 1958 the RAF's Flying Manual (AP129) directed pilots to abandon the aircraft if spin recovery was not effected by 3,000 feet above ground level for elementary trainers and 8,000 feet for advanced trainers.

Stall: an aircraft stalls when the smooth flow over its wings becomes turbulent and the lift decreases. Essentially, pilots investigate the condition in order to recognise its onset, the aim being to restore the lift with minimum height loss.

Standard Beam Approach (SBA): in essence, a radar landing aid which transmitted a 30 mile long, very narrow radio beam down the extended centreline of the runway. This told a pilot receiving the aural 'on-the-beam' signal that he was somewhere along the projected centre line of the runway. To furnish an exact location *along* the beam, an 'Outer Marker' radio beacon was sited at a known distance from touchdown. This sent a coded signal vertically upwards to tell an inbound pilot that he should commence his final approach, descending at a rate of 600 feet a minute until he heard the Inner Marker (effectively at touchdown), and either saw the airfield and landed, or climbed away and had another think.

Stick (control column): from the 1950s, certainly, this was always the preferred term among pilots; 'pole' was equally acceptable but somewhat informal, 'joystick' almost antediluvially archaic, and 'control column' too pedantic even for Central Flying School. So stick it is, even where the aircraft in question had a wheel, or a yoke.

Wreck: a misnomer employed by air-crash enthusiasts seeking an elegant variation on 'air crash'. Any class of aircraft may be wrecked if it is on the ground but the nautical model, though legitimately transferred in the railway context, is misemployed for machines which come to grief in flight. Notwithstanding this, mainstream aviation usage accepts wreckage as a synonym for debris.

Yards/Metres: again, let purists go pale, but to the workaday walker these are interchangeable up to half a mile or so.

Acknowledgements

To the pioneering, joint authors of the two *Dark Peak Aircraft Wreck* books (1979 and 1982) who paved the way for all walkers puzzled by metal fragments chanced upon while traversing the Peakland Moors. To Ron Collier 1935–2011: Ranger Phil Shaw, a field companion, remembers how Ron tramped the moors in the 1970s 'with nothing but a compass, hearsay, and myths to go on, so that locating a wreck often took him weeks'; additionally, Ron devoted twenty-five years to the Air Training Corps and qualified as a private pilot. He had intended to cover the White Peak, but ill health intervened. To Roni Wilkinson, who, as an author of boys' stories, set the tone for Ron's findings, serialising the material in the *Barnsley Chronicle* and subsequently joining Pen & Sword Books Ltd.

To veteran air-crash researchers John Ownsworth and Alan Jones (a noted aviation artist), both of whom furnished much extra-archival detail.

To Malcolm Barrass, whose superlative website *Air of Authority* (www.rafweb.org) is a never-failing and utterly dependable source.

To Clive Teale, aviator and grammarian, for technical advice. Similarly to Ken Johnson and Ken Clare for down-to-earth criticism.

To Mr Ian Burgess, of Bury, who supplied 'links' enabling the quality of enthusiast web-forum observations to be assessed. To Professor Séan Moran, of Wirksworth, who did the same, and then proved an engaging field-work companion.

To the several hundred folk interviewed, particularly from busy farming families, who gave their time to the research for this series.

To the RAF Museum – and particularly to Andrew Dennis; also to the Imperial War Museum and the British Library for assistance with transcribing wartime map references to modern coordinates.

To the photographic staff at ASDA, Spondon, who, if irreverent, gave unstinting assistance; similarly, to the staff at the co-located McDonalds, for sustenance.

To the Chief Executive of Derwent Living, winter 2010–11 (the coldest in 100 years): for no central heating, and memorable proof-reading in fingerless gloves.

To the traced copyright holders authorising the use of their photographs: Richard Haigh, manager, intellectual properties, Rolls-Royce; Nicola Hunt, intellectual property rights copyright unit, MOD; archives staff, Imperial War Museum; Judy Nokes, licensing adviser, HMSO (Crown Copyright/MOD); John Ownsworth, for photographs used by Ron Collier; Archives staff, Royal Air Force Museum; Mike Stowe, American crash reports; Julian Temple, archivist, Vickers' Brooklands Museum, Weybridge. Craving the indulgence of those for whom all contact attempts have failed.

Despite such inestimable assistance, any errors remaining, and all opinions expressed, are my own.

Pat Cunningham, DFM

Selective References

Air Ministry (1941) *Air Navigation Volume 1, AP1234.* London: HMSO

Air Ministry (1943) *Elementary Flying Training, AP1979A.* London: HMSO

Air Ministry (1948) *The Rise and Fall of the German Air Force (1931 to 1945).* London: HMSO

Air Ministry (1954) *Flying, Volumes 1 and 2, AP129.* (Sixth edition). London: HMSO

Air Ministry (1960) *Flying Instructor's Handbook,* AP3225D. London: HMSO

Air Ministry (1960) *Pilot's Notes Vampire T.11.* London: HMSO

Barrass, Malcolm (2005) *Air of Authority* (www.rafweb.org), (RAF organisation)

Bennett, D. C. T. (1936) *The Complete Air Navigator.* London: Pitman

Boylan, Marshall S. (1992) *A Moorland Dedication.* Leek: William Beech

Collier, Ron; Wilkinson, Roni. (1979 1982) *Dark Peak Aircraft Wrecks 1 & 2.* Barnsley: Pen & Sword

Cunningham, Pat (Peakland Aircrashes Series: *The South* (2005); *The Central Area* (2006); *The North* (2006). Ashbourne: Landmark Publishing

Fellowes, P. F. M. (1942) *Britain's Wonderful Air Force.* London: Odhams

Giddings, Malcolm L. (1984) *RAF Lichfield & Church Broughton.* Ashbourne: Colerne Debden

Hammerton, J. (1943) *ABC of the RAF.* London: Amalgamated Press

Handley Page Ltd (1949) *Forty Years On.* London: Handley Page

HMSO (1937) *RAF Pocket Handbook,1937.* London: Air Ministry

HMSO. (1942-1943) *Aircraft Recognition.* London: Sampson Clark

Jordanoff, Assen. (1941) *Safety in Flight.* New York: Funk & Wagnalls

Lamplugh, A. G. (1931) *Accidents in Civil Aviation.* Royal Aeronautical Paper, Institution of Aeronautical Engineers, 29 October 1931, London

Monday, David. (1994) *Hamlyn Concise Guide to British Aircraft of World War 11.* London: Chancellor Press

Office of Public Sector Information (OPSI) 2008. *Protection of Military Remains Act 1986, order 2008.* London

Ogilvy, David. (1977) *Bleriot to Spitfire.* (Shuttleworth) Shrewsbury: Airlife

Saville-Sneath, R.A. (1945) *Aircraft of the United States, Volume One.* London: Penguin

Phelps, Anthony. (1944) *I couldn't care less (*Air Transport Auxiliary*).* Leicester: Harborough

Stewart, Oliver. (1941) *The Royal Air Force in Pictures.* London: Country Life

Sturtivant, Ray; Page, Gordon. (1999) *'Air Britain Listings' series.* Old Woking: Unwin

Thetford, Owen (1958) *Aircraft of the Royal Air Force 1918-58.* London: Putnam

OTHER BOOKS BY THE AUTHOR

Non-fiction
Peakland Aircrashes Series:
The South (2005)
The Central Area (2006)
The North (2006)

High Peak Air Crash Sites, Central Region

Bomb on the Red Markers

Faction
A Magnificent Diversion Series (Acclaimed by the First World War Aviation Historical
    Society)
The Infinite Reaches 1915-16
Contact Patrol 1916
Sold A Pup 1917
The Great Disservice 1918

Blind Faith: Joan Waste, Derby's Martyr
Joyce Lewis, Lichfield's feisty Martyr

Fiction
In Kinder's Mists (a Kinderscout ghost story)
Though the Treason Pleases (Irish Troubles)